INVISIBLE AGENTS OF CREATION

INVISIBLE AGENTS OF CREATION

IMPLICATIONS OF COSMIC PATTERNS

FRED CAMERON

LUMINARIA PRESS

Formerly titled *The Universe Is Fake (and what to do about it)*

Typeset in Minion and Myriad

Luminaria Press
Port Gamble, WA 98364

Printed in the United States of America

Library of Congress Control Number: 2013905284

ISBN: 978-0-9657104-5-9

CONTENTS

LIST OF FIGURES

1

INTRODUCTION

$\mathcal{W}$E LIVE IN an amazing part of the universe. In fact, as we'll see, it's a little too amazing to have been created by random clouds of swirling gasses, gravity and molten rock, which is the current scientific theory of how our Solar System came into being. But if we look closer it's hard to avoid the conclusion that, at least, the Sun, Moon and Earth were constructed to be as they are for our benefit. The evidence extends, in fact, to the very bedrock of modern physics. Somebody has diddled with our universe. Modified it. Created patterns in it that couldn't possibly have occurred by chance. This, as we will see, constitutes a message to us that the universe is not what it seems to be, and therefore by extension, we who exist within it are not what we seem to be either.

Solar System Weirdness

Which puts us in a predicament. If we're living in a Mel Brooks, *Blazing Saddles* sort of universe, who created it, and why? The idea of a crafted universe is very old. The religions like to stipulate a God of various descriptions, but this doesn't really explain anything, comsidering the evidence we'll look at, so the idea of some new kind of Agency—and we're going to call it just that—may explain a bit more. But evidence first; theories second. We'll want to take a look at what we've got before drawing any definite conclusions.

So first, using some simple numbers from up-to-the-minute astronomical observations, and even a bit of quantum physics, we'll find ourselves slipping very quickly into inexplicable weirdness that extends far beyond what science can explain. To start, simple observations, which we will run through, show that the Sun, our own planet Earth, and the Moon couldn't have randomly gotten the way they are. They were purposely adjusted and tweaked to be the way we find them.

But that's not all. Our own physical bodies have also been "tuned" to our local solar environment as if to say that we ourselves are part of these same patterns, and are caught up in them. These patterns appear inescapably to be a message meant specifically for us.

If a message has been arranged for us to find, then some Agency left it. The first question that arises—Who are or were they?—turns out to not be as important as: What does the message mean for us, to whom it has been sent? These questions will have to wait until we read the message and then decipher what it says.

The message consists of a small set of numerical measurements that form patterns that just shouldn't exist in a natural environment. These numbers require no more than high school algebra to find, and indeed most of them are well-known; some of the others are not. None of them, though, are of interest to professional scientists who feel there are much more important problems worthy of their attention, so these facts just sit in books and Wikis, waiting for someone to notice them and put them together, which is what I propose to do here. Data first—nothing too complicated—speculations on what it all might mean afterward.

The first part of the message, and the biggest, stares us in the face every night.

2

THE EVIDENCE

THE MOST AMAZING astronomical fact known to us is visible in the sky nearly every period of twenty-four hours, but especially during total solar eclipses. From our vantage point on Earth, the Sun and Moon appear to be exactly the same size. During a total solar eclipse, the Moon exactly covers the disk of the Sun.

Figure 1

Can anything explain this? The Sun is 400 times the size of the Moon, yet is 400 times farther away, so their apparent sizes are the same. In the eighteenth century, the meaning of this fact was widely debated by astronomers, but today if it is mentioned to astronomy students at all it's just called coincidental. Nobody wants to talk about it, because nobody can explain it.

Figure 2 shows the Earth and Moon to scale, both to size and distance. This unusual picture can give us a bit more of a visceral feel for sizes and distances than can the more usual diagrams which are rarely shown to scale. Perhaps this is because little surface detail can be seen on either body. The Earth is 7920 miles across, and the Moon 2160. They are about 235,000 miles apart, so they each must be shown very small to see them accurately on the same page.

Even so, it's almost possible to see a human scale here. Does this picture come alive for you in some sense? We stand on Earth's surface and look up at the Moon. Men have traveled to the Moon.

The more I look at this picture, though, the more I wonder how the Moon can just hang there. Of course, there are physical laws for orbital motion and gravity, but as we'll see later, we might wish they explained a bit more than they do. But back to eclipses for the moment.

During a solar eclipse, the Sun would be far past the Moon (about 230 feet past at this scale), directly in line with the Moon, and would cast the Moon's long, thin shadow directly toward Earth, where it would cover a spot approximately a hundred miles or less across on the surface at any instant. The shadow is shown highlighted in Figure 3 so you can see it. If you were standing within that area on Earth's surface, the apparent sizes of the Sun and Moon would be the same.

Seen like this, to scale, how likely do you think it is that this exact arrangement of Earth, Moon and Sun could have all happened by chance—their relative sizes and distances from each other—in order to bring the point of this shadow so exactly to Earth's surface? It's extremely unlikely. The odds against this arrangement are, well, astronomical. Look at the graphic again. The shadow looks like an arrow pointing directly at the Earth. A very precise, very targeted, long-distance arrow.

Is this configuration coincidental? Are there more apparent "coincidences" regarding the Earth and the Moon that might help us decide? Indeed there are. And when these are stacked up beside one another, the chance they could all be coincidental becomes remote—so remote as to be essentially impossible. Let's look at some of them.

Two Dancing Partners

If we compare the size of the Moon with the size of the Earth, we find that the Earth is 3.66 times as big as the Moon. Taking the reciprocal, the Moon

Figure 2   Figure 3

is .273 times as large as the Earth. We are going to find these two numbers—perhaps with the decimal point in different places—repeated over and over, sometimes in the sky, but sometimes here on Earth and in our own bodies. In information theory, repetition creates patterns that change raw numbers from mere noise into something meaningful. We're going to be on the lookout for such patterns.

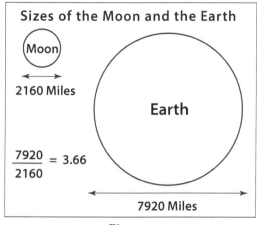

Next item. If we take that 3.66 as 366 we find that this is the number of full rotations of the Earth in one Earth year. Which may need an explanation, since we know one year has only 365¼ days. The explanation lies in how the day is defined. We measure one day, technically called one mean solar day, to be the time between when the Sun is at its zenith (its highest point overhead) on two consecutive days. This day has exactly 24 hours by definition and is used to measure common civil time. 365¼ mean solar days make one year. (The word "mean" means "average." The Sun doesn't actually appear to move the same amount each day during the year, so astronomers devised an "average" or "mean" solar day to make timekeeping easier.)

Another type of day, one which is commonly used in astronomy, is the sidereal day, which is defined as the time between two successive appearances of a bright star in the same position overhead. In other words, a full turn of the Earth measured against the background stars. This day is only 23 hours, 56 minutes and 4 seconds long—236 seconds shorter than a mean solar day. The movement of the Earth around the Sun accounts for the difference; the Earth has to turn farther to point again at the Sun than it does to point again at the same star, which makes the solar day a bit longer than the sidereal day. By the time the Earth has returned to the same position in its orbit around the Sun—one year, these 236 seconds per day have added up to almost exactly one additional full day, one additional full rotation, making 366 full rotations in one year.

Let's compare the length of these days. The number of seconds in one mean solar day of exactly 24 hours is 24 times 60 minutes per hour times 60 seconds per minute, which comes to 86,400 seconds. A sidereal day is 236 seconds shorter: 86,164 seconds. The percent by which the sidereal day is shorter than a mean solar day is found by taking their difference, 236 seconds, and dividing by 86,400, which comes to .273%. Oh, no. Here's another 273, which is our other pattern number. Let's just note it for now, though, and take stock.

We can say there are 366 actual days in a year, and the Earth is 3.66 times the size of the Moon. The same digits appear in each of these numbers. There is no reason why this should be so; it just is. The Moon is 27.3% the size of the Earth, and a sidereal day on Earth is .273% shorter than a mean solar day. Odd, but if this was all, it probably wouldn't mean anything. But we're attempting to show that there is a meaningful pattern of numerical relationships among the Sun, the Moon and the Earth that just shouldn't be if the Solar System evolved in a natural, random way. And we're just getting started. (All the numbers we're going to find are summarized in the Appendix.)

Moonstruck

Next, we observe that the Moon rotates around the Earth once every 27.32 days. This is called the sidereal period of the Moon, and is the amount of time it takes the Moon to return to the same place in the heavens as measured against the background of the fixed stars. (This is a different measure than the period from Full Moon to Full Moon, which is longer, 29.5 days, called the Moon's synodic period.)

One sidereal lunar month is 27.32 Earth days long. And the Moon is 27.3% the size of the Earth. Two, seven, three. We have the same digits again. Well, that's interesting. It could be a coincidence or it could really be a pattern.

Our strange Moon

Let's look closer at the Moon. 27.32 Earth days is one lunar day from the point of view of the Moon. One lunar day is the time between two successive passages of the Sun directly overhead at a point on the Moon's surface. For our Moon, the sidereal day and sidereal month are the same, since the Moon keeps the same face towards Earth in its orbit; one full orbit around the Earth takes exactly the same time as one rotation on its axis. The Moon rotates once on its axis every 27.32 days: therefore, one lunar day is also 27.32 Earth days.

One more look. If we add 366 of these lunar days together they equal 10,000 Earth days. (366 x 27.32 = 10,000.) This is a consequence of 3.66 and .2732 being reciprocal numbers, but it sets up a "construction" constant of 10,000 that we will see again later on when we look at Earth's orbit around the Sun.

Are there more apparent "coincidences" that contain these same numbers? Indeed there are, and many of them, apparently, have nothing to do with planets and moons. As they start to accumulate, we may begin to wonder if there really is some pattern, some meaning to them. Perhaps they should not be treated as coincidences at all. For now we'll just keep lining them up before we start speculating about what significance they might carry. They're not all in the sky, so let's look more closely at the environment that surrounds us right here on Earth. We'll start with water and how its temperature is measured.

The Temperature of Nothing

The temperature scale used in physics (and in most of Europe) is the Centigrade or Celsius scale, named after the nineteenth century Swedish astronomer Anders Celsius who invented it. 0°C was defined as the ice point of water, the temperature where water freezes. 100°C was defined as the boiling point of water—the point where liquid water turns to steam. (The corresponding range in the Fahrenheit scale used in the United States is 32° to 212°.) One hundred Centigrade degrees therefore define the three conditions or states of water: solid ice, liquid water, and gaseous steam. Therefore, the Centigrade temperature scale implicitly carries within it an echo of the properties of water.

Temperature itself is defined as the statistical average kinetic energy of molecules in a substance (which is just a fun way of saying the energy of movement due to heat). This measures how fast the molecules are moving; a higher temperature means the molecules are moving faster with more energy. For example, "room temperature" refers to the average energy of movement of the air molecules in a room that is at a temperature comfortable to humans. Now, there exists a certain very low temperature at which all such random thermal movement ceases (except for a bit of quantum wiggling, but that's something that won't concern us). This temperature is called absolute zero and is numerically equal to -273.2°C. This number expresses a quantitative relationship between the energy points of the three states of water and the energy point where no molecular motion exists in *any* substance. Note that our familiar digits appear again in this number: 273.2.

There is a temperature scale used by physicists that takes -273.2°C as its own zero mark; this is the Kelvin temperature scale, named after William Thompson, known as Lord Kelvin, a physicist at the turn of the nineteenth century. On the Kelvin scale, the freezing point of water is +273.2°K; this is just another way of saying 0° Centigrade. This scale is useful for very low temperatures such as those found in certain laboratory experiments; it is also used by astrophysicists to express the temperature of stars. And it's used to express the color temperature of ordinary light bulbs, which is of special interest to photographers.

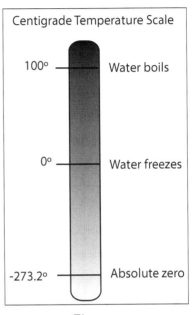

Figure 5

Can this have anything to do with the Moon? Or with the fact that the Moon is 27.3% the size of the Earth? These are just numbers.

Pure coincidence, you say, that the freezing point of water, 273.2°K, could be in any way related to the sidereal period of the Moon, 27.32 days. They don't measure the same thing; they aren't even the same number—one is ten times the other, disregarding the units, which are incompatible in any event.

But all right. We have 273.2°K and 27.32 days in a sidereal month. Suppose we take ten lunar months to get 273.2 days so that both numbers match numerically. What might 273.2 days signify?

Mothers and Babies

273 days is the average human gestation period from conception to birth. This corresponds very closely to nine calendar months, usually taken as 273 or 274 days. Our bodies are around 70% water, but the womb is its

own watery domain, and in many cultures, the Moon is a feminine symbol. Using our lateral thinking abilities we can easily connect ten lunar sidereal months or nine calendar months, with the time a woman carries her child to term. (In addition, 27+ days, of course, is very close to the average female menstrual cycle.)

We have a circle or web of ideas here that are beginning to form another pattern: the sidereal period of the Moon, the human female gestation period, the womb as a watery domain, water itself, the freezing temperature of water, and back to the sidereal period of the Moon. There is something rational about this. It shouldn't mean anything, yet it does somewhere inside us. But why should it revolve around the seemingly arbitrary number, 237.2? Let's go on and try to expand this circle of ideas and connections to see if we can find out why.

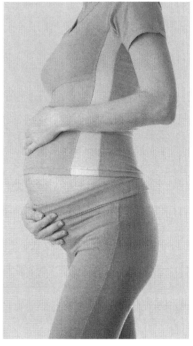

Figure 6

It's a Gas!

Next item. According to experiments done by the Frenchman Gay-Lussac in 1802, if the quantity and pressure of a gas are held constant, then the volume of the gas increases linearly as its temperature rises. This physical law was named after him; it was later called the ideal gas law. If you imagine this gas in a very light container that can easily expand in size as the gas is heated, you have the picture. As the temperature of the gas goes up, the molecules move faster (their kinetic energy increases) and they whack the sides of the container harder, making it expand. What interests us is that gasses expand or contract by 1/273.2 of their volume for every Centigrade degree of heating or cooling. This is either meaningless or mind-blowing.

In the ideal gas law we have all wrapped up in one the ideas of absolute zero, the freezing and boiling points of water, the size of the Moon compared to Earth and the Moon's sidereal period. So far. Now, water in the form of steam could be the gas in question, but so could any other gas.

But those dag gone 273.2s just keep rolling in. There is no obvious reason why another one should appear here; there doesn't seem to be any connection. It just does.

Cosmic Patterns, Baby

Next item. An important observation made in the last few decades is the presence of a cosmic radiation that comes uniformly from all directions in space. This radiation was once thought to be the remnant of the so-called Big Bang, but it's *too* uniform. The nature of this radiation as observed does not fit the requirements of the Big Bang theory, and is one of the reasons this theory is currently in decline. This radiation exists, nevertheless, and is now thought to have to do with magnetic fields in plasmas, which are huge concentrations of charged particles that exist throughout space.

In measuring the energy of radiation of this nature, it is customary in physics to use a temperature scale, and the Kelvin scale is best suited for this task. The temperature of the background microwave radiation is 2.73°K, just a bit above absolute zero. We have that same number, now in a different context. What is interesting is that the same *numerical value* has occurred once again—our old pattern number.

March Madness!

Let's bring the Sun into the picture. Consider the Sun as one gigantic gymnasium. You can line up 109.3 Earth-sized basketballs across the diameter of the Sun (Figure 7).

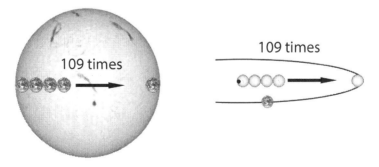

Figure 7   Figure 8

Now consider the orbit of the Earth as an even larger gym, with the Sun exactly at mid-court. You can line up 109.3 Sun-sized basketballs from mid-court to the edge of the court, making a sort of fractal Solar System pattern (Figure 8).

In the first case, 109.3 Earths fit side-by-side inside the Sun. In the second case, 109.3 Suns fit in the Earth's orbital radius. The Sun doesn't have to be the size it is. The Earth doesn't have to be the size it is, either. It doesn't have to be the distance from the Sun that it is. But there you are. Look up the numbers and get out your pocket calculator. Also, note that 109.3 is 4 x 27.32(!)—something we'll come back to in the last chapter.

On the other hand, maybe the Sun, Earth and Moon are the sizes and distances they are for a reason.

Squares and Circles

There is one more fundamental appearance of the digits 2732 we need to note. Consider a square of two units length on each side as shown in Figure 9. Draw a circle inside the square; the cir-

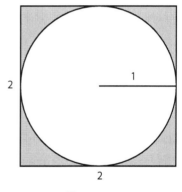

cle will have a radius of 1 unit. The area of the square is 4 and the area of the circle is πr^2 which equals just π or 3.1416 since r = 1. What is the difference in area between the square and the circle? It is $4 - \pi$. This is represented by the shaded area in the diagram. Finally we ask what fraction of the area of the circle is this shaded area? It would be the shaded area $(4 - \pi)$ divided by the area of the circle, π. Using a calculator to solve the expression $(4 - \pi)$

Figure 9

/ π we get 0.2732 to four decimal places. Here are the same digits we have already seen many times. The same exact digits we have seen above now appear as a pure, dimensionless number, for whatever units we used in our measurements cancel out. This diagram doesn't appear to be connected to the Moon, the Earth, water or babies; it is more abstract and probably more fundamental.

Based on this fact, organic chemist Peter Plichta in his book *God's Secret Formula*[1] says that the number 0.2732 must be a new mathematical constant, never before discovered. But we have seen the same sequence of digits describe temperature based on the properties of water, the sidereal period of the Moon and the human gestation period. Are these phenomena related to the same mathematical constant? What sort of undiscovered universal "constant" would govern the human gestation period? Are there some construction parameters that govern the orbital period of the Moon or the sizes of the Earth and Moon? Could these same parameters govern the properties of water and the temperature of absolute zero?

This all must be some kind of trick! Where did all these 273s come from? Never mind the presence of a decimal point in the pattern. The Earth. The Moon. The Sun. Solar eclipses. Temperature relative to the properties of water. The human gestation period. The ratio of the area of a square to an inscribed circle—simple geometry. Numerical and visual "coincidences," all mediated by the digits 2732 or its inverse, 366.

Notice that none of the numbers we have used depend on the units the numbers are expressed in, except for the Earth day. Even the temperatures we used only depend on dividing the difference between the freezing and boiling points of water into 100 equal units. There is no explanation why these things should be so. We could write one or two of them off to coincidence, but not all of them.

If only the Moon just wasn't hanging up there, exactly the same apparent size as the Sun.

What's going on?

Everybody's Got Sol, Baby

There is more here to discover. Repeating the same procedure with perimeters instead of areas yields the same result: $(4 - \pi) / \pi$. What geometrical principle or relation is being displayed here, and what does it have to do with the Earth and Moon?

There's more. What if the circle and square were instead a sphere inscribed inside a cube—a three-dimensional diagram? Calculating the surface areas, subtracting and finding the ratio of excess amount (the eight curved corners between cube and sphere) to the surface area of the sphere, the result is $(6 - \pi) / \pi$. The same result is obtained using volumes instead of surface areas. The result is 0.9099 in each case. This number didn't correlate to anything, nor did its square or square root. But its reciprocal was 1.0991, and this number did look familiar. Remember the basketballs? Multiply this number by 100, it comes to 109.91, which is extremely close

21

to the number of Earths that fit inside the Sun's diameter, which was 109.3. The two numbers are off by about a half percent, but the diameter of the Sun cannot be determined exactly as it has no hard surface, so the two numbers are sensibly the same.

But what did these two ratios mean? The ratio of the sizes of the Earth and Moon are related to a circle inscribed in a square, and the ratio of the sizes of the Sun and Earth are related to a sphere inscribed in a cube if the reciprocal is taken and the factor 100 kicked in. We will encounter 100 later in connection with the Sun, but why is it needed here? Besides being a scale factor, might it have another meaning? No one knows.

Is the Sun/Earth somehow the reciprocal of the Earth/Moon? Is the factor 100 related somehow to going from two dimensions to three dimensions? Does this imply some sort of dimensional "type" difference when the Sun is considered? The word "type" is used in the sense of the Sun being of a fundamentally different type of entity than the Earth or Moon. It is true that the Sun is fundamentally different, but how might this be enfolded differently in circles and squares versus spheres and cubes?

While we're looking at the Sun, we shouldn't forget to note that sunspots move across the face of the Sun with a period called the Carrington Rotation. It's 27.3 days.

I know. What's going on?

Speculation Sidebar

It may be that no one knows why .273—found from a circle in a square—is a characteristic pattern number of our local cosmos, but that's no reason we can't speculate a bit. Look back at that diagram of the circle and square. Let's imagine the circle by itself first. To the ancient Greeks, a circle was the perfect shape, symbolic of an ideal world, the world of the long-lost Golden Age.

The heavenly, perfect circle morphs into an imperfect, earthly square

Imagine now grabbing hold of that circle and pulling out or unfolding from its center four sharp corners as flaps to form the square. The square has always been symbolic of the material realm, the ordinary world, which as we all know, is a far cry from any sort of ideal world. The transformation from circle to square—the appearance of those four gray corners behind the circle, is symbolic of an ontological shift from a more perfect to a less perfect realm, from the Golden Age to our present age. It would be natural, therefore, for .273 and its reciprocal 3.66 to be characteristic factors in our current world.

Remember that we arrived at .273 by comparing the newly-exposed gray corners with the original circle. Does this shift correspond to any planet-wide event? We will see later on that it does. A cataclysm of some kind about 12,000 years ago ended a global Golden Age, which has been recounted in many myths and legends from around the world. This same event also corresponded to a dramatic shift in human consciousness.

So in many ways, as we're seeing, .273 and 3.66 are indeed markers of our modern age.

Leonardo da Vinci's Circle and Square

Many people are familiar with the drawing in Figure 10 known as the Vitruvian Man. It depicts two men of ideal proportions superimposed on one another. It is loosely based on earlier work by a Roman architect named Vitruvius who lived in the first century BCE. Besides the superposition, Leonardo added the circle and square. Nobody seems to question where the circle and square came from, and why they are the sizes they are. They have nothing to do with Vitruvius, only with Leonardo. Yes, they touch the hands and feet of the figures, but the upper set of arms could have been drawn higher, say, which would change their relationship. Why these *particular* circles and squares?

Vitruvian Man

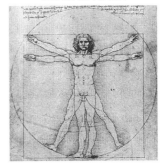

Figure 10

According to the WikiPedia article on *Vitruvian Man*, we are told that

"Leonardo envisaged the great picture chart of the human body he had produced through his anatomical drawings and Vitruvian Man as a *cosmografia del minor mondo* (cosmography of the microcosm). He believed the workings of the human body to be an analogy for the workings of the universe."

There is much more to this last idea than at first meets the eye. For if we stack two circles that represent the Earth and Moon on top of each other, to scale and drawn to match the man's height, as shown in Figure 11-a, a new sort of picture is revealed. The larger circle that encompasses them both exactly matches the square Leonardo drew.

Leonardo's Square

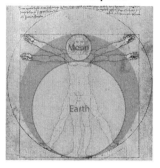

Figure 11-a

It is facile to assume Leonardo did not know this. Surely it's a major part of the human body as "an analogy for the workings of the universe." Cosmography is a description and interpretation of the visible universe. In philosophy, it is the science dealing with the whole order of nature. Leonardo, therefore, is perhaps showing us that the order of the universe is based on, or intimately connected with, us as human beings, of which his drawn figures are symbolic.

Let's redraw our Earth-plus-Moon circles a bit larger so they match Leonardo's circle, as shown in Figure 11-b. Now we see why he drew the upper arms in the position we see them; they define this Earth-plus-Moon circle exactly. Is it significant, for example, that here Earth and Moon join exactly where man's brain is? (This is also where the third eye or *ajna* chakra is located.) Are we to think about them together in some sense, of which this drawing is some sort of abstract hint? Leonardo concealed much in his art, and he certainly couldn't draw actual Earth and Moon circles without getting a knock on the door from the Inquisition. So let's look at this drawing more closely.

Leonardo's Large Circle

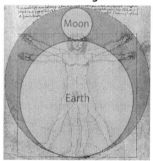

Figure 11-b

Look first at just the man with his arms straight out and feet together. He just fits inside the square; his genitals are at the exact center of this square. A horizontal line through his navel, though, forms a rectangle down to his feet that has a width to height ratio of φ, the Golden Mean, a ratio that was used by many different Renaissance artists to determine the relations among the elements in their paintings; Leonardo used it over and over again. The second man with more upraised arms and spread legs describes the circle Leonardo drew; its center is the man's navel. Inside this circle I've shown the Earth and Moon to scale. This diagram is sometimes shown with the Moon sitting on the man's head, which isn't strictly correct. As noted, there is more about this drawing to "think" about than first meets the eye. Above all, though, the tips of the upper fingers link the circle macrocosm of Earth and Moon with the microcosm of man himself—which, we are going to see as we go along, really is an analogy for the "workings of the universe."

Fee, Phi, Fo, Fum

There is another traditional way to place man in the cosmos. The diagram in Figure 12 is from Cornelius Agrippa and depicts man superimposed on a pentagram, a five-pointed star. We are not as interested in Agrippa's attribution of the seven "planets" known to the ancients as we are in repeating the previous operations with a circle inscribed in a square. This time let's look at a circle inscribed in a pentagram. The motivation for this is to try to tie in the Golden Section constant Phi or φ (which has a numerical value of 1.618…) with our familiar constants 2.73 and 366. φ appears by itself many times in a pentagram as the ratio of the lengths of the various chords in the

Figure 12

figure, but I wanted to find all three numbers in the same diagram, using exactly the same procedure as before.

The most common arrangement is to inscribe the pentagram inside a circle, which is what Agrippa did. This, however, is not what we did before; we need the circle to be inside the pentagram in some manner. There are clearly two ways to inscribe a circle in a pentagram. The rim of the circle could be drawn as shown in Figure 13, or could be drawn just slightly larger so the circumference touched the inner angles of the star. This last method didn't work, but the method shown in the diagram did.

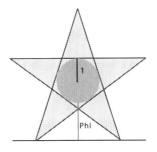

Figure 13

We need to subtract the area of the circle from the area of the pentagon and then divide the result by the area of the circle. This doesn't appear to make any geometric sense, but after several pages of geometrical constructions and equations I arrived at an answer of 2.742. Well, this was very close to our 2.732, but not really close enough, so I wanted to know how far off it was. The usual procedure here is to take the difference between the standard answer and the found answer and divide by the standard answer, thus: (2.742 − 2.732) / 2.732. Times 100, this gives the percentage error. The result is .366% off. Exactly. We essentially just have the reciprocal of 2.732 adjusted by a few factors of ten, but still the difference had to be exactly the size it was to get the 366 error factor.

And, as you can see, dropping a vertical from the rim of the circle to a line between any two of the legs gives us our φ in the same diagram.

Elevensies and Other Oddities

We pause to note one other naturally-occurring number that is close to our .273. The fraction 3/11 is 0.272727… where the ellipsis means the 27s repeat indefinitely. Rounded to three decimal places this comes to .273. The reciprocal of this number is 11/3 or 3.6666… where again the 6s repeat. These are very close to our numbers .273 and 3.66. They are not exactly the same, because the expression (4 − π) / π that we found earlier in relation to a circle inscribed in a square to eight decimals is 0.27323954. This may be significant or not—either that they are so close as to be sensibly the same numbers, or that they are off by some perhaps meaningful fraction. In any event, using either .273 number, we can generate some interesting relationships. There are 360° in a circle.Remembering our fraction 11/3:

- 360 x 11 = 3960, which is the radius of the Earth in miles.
- 360 x 3 = 1080, which is the radius of the Moon in miles.
- 360 x 12 = 4320, which is 1/100 the radius of the Sun in miles, thrown in for good measure.

How is it that the sizes of the Earth, Sun and Moon are related to each other by simple integer factors? What is the *cause* of these relations? Are we seeing the hand of some construction company, some orb architect? Johannes Kepler, who we will meet in the next section, said, "Geometry existed before the creation." So—we can add—did mathematics, at least in our corner of the universe. But again, why? What caused all these mathematical patterns, all these non-random numbers? To see if we can find out why, let's expand our viewpoint by taking a few trips around the Sun.

The Earth and the Sun

Physics and astronomy are strewn with interrelated numbers and ratios that have no official, rational relationship to one another, yet which seem mysteriously significant, especially when considered together. So we will look at one final set of relationships, using no more than a sprinkling of high school algebra in order to get an idea of its scope, so fear not. Let's take a look.

Johannes Kepler formulated his three laws of planetary motion in the early seventeenth century, based on an analysis of the observations of Mars that Tycho Brahe had made some years before. The first law says the orbit of each planet is an ellipse with the Sun at one focus. The second law says the line joining the planet to the Sun sweeps out equal areas in equal times, which just means that a planet moves slightly faster in its orbit when it is closest to the Sun than when it's farther away.

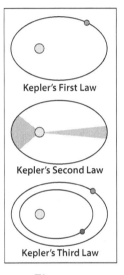

Kepler's First Law

Kepler's Second Law

Kepler's Third Law

Figure 14

It is the third law which will be of interest to us; it says the square of the period of a planet (the period is the length of time the planet takes to make one complete revolution around the Sun) is directly proportional to the cube of its mean distance from the Sun. Never mind the squares and cubes. Simply stated, this means planets further from the Sun will travel slower in their orbits than will those closer in, and this law describes the exact relationship. In fact, if we know one planet's distance to the Sun and its period, those factors for any other planet can easily be calculated. So for example, since we know the distance of the Earth to the Sun, and the Earth's period, we can calculate the period of any other planet if we know its distance from the Sun also.

Kepler's third law has an alternate form which will be of more use to us. With some simple algebra, the equation can be stated as "the planets' distances from the Sun are inversely proportional to the squares of their orbital velocities." In short, every unique distance from the Sun has a definite orbital velocity. Every planet in the Solar System obeys this law. The mass or the size of the planet doesn't matter; only its distance from the Sun. (Note that nobody knows why this is. We have formulas from Kepler and Newton that describe motion under the influence of gravity, but this is

quite different than knowing what gravity *is*. Even Newton wouldn't speculate. He wrote down his descriptive equations and was done with it. Note
well though, a description isn't an explanation.) In this form, if we know
both the orbital velocity and distance from the Sun, we can find the orbital
velocity of any other planet if we know its distance.

In any event, this form of Kepler's law is what we want, because we are
first going to look at how fast the Earth travels around the Sun and then use
the third law to do some exploring.

The distance from the Earth to the Sun varies from 91.4 to 94.5 million miles, since the Earth's orbit is not circular but is slightly elliptical, as
per Kepler's first law. It is closest to the Sun during winter in the Northern
hemisphere and farthest during summer. We'll average this distance to 93
million miles, keeping in mind that there will be a small plus-or-minus in
our calculations. The circumference of the orbit is calculated by multiplying this amount by 2π. The result is 584,340,000 miles give or take. This
distance is traveled in one year or 365.26 days (the Earth's period), so the

*Faster than a
Ferrari*

orbital velocity comes to 18.52 miles per second give
or take, once days have been converted to seconds.
(This is about 67,000 miles per hour.)

We pause here to note two facts. First, the diameter of the Earth's orbit
(i.e. twice its distance to the Sun) is 186,000,000 miles, again give or take.
The speed of light is 186,300 miles per second. True, the units are different,
but we're still looking for numerical patterns without regard to units or
the decimal place. If we had used a slightly different Earth-Sun distance of
93.15 million miles—still well within the actual range, the diameter of the
Earth's orbit would be 186,300,000. We can calculate the time light takes
to traverse the diameter of Earth's orbit, and we get very close to 1,000
seconds or about 16 2/3 minutes.

The second and related fact is the orbital velocity of 18.52 miles per
second. Actually, it is in the range from 18.20 to 18.82 miles per second,
depending on how far the Earth is from the Sun at the moment. Remember,
Kepler's second law says a planet moves faster when its closer to the Sun
and slower when its farther away. Admittedly cherry-picking 18.63 from
within this range—but with good reason as we'll see later, we multiply this
number by 10,000 and obtain the speed of light. Here we see that "construction" constant of 10,000 again. At this point, it is worth asking the
question: Why should the Earth's orbital velocity be one ten-thousandth of
the speed of light? And, moreover, why should light also take 1000 seconds

to cross Earth's orbit? Hold those questions (and objections!) for a bit.

As a check on our work, let's now use Kepler's third law to calculate the orbital velocity of Mars. This works out to be 15 miles per second. Mars is farther from the Sun, so its orbital speed is correspondingly less than Earth's. Mercury, the closest planet to the Sun, moves around the Sun at nearly 30 miles per second.

Next, we would like to use the same law to answer the following question: What would be the orbital speed of a hypothetical planet positioned exactly at the surface of the Sun? In other words, the nearer a planet is to the Sun, the faster it moves. The actual surface of the Sun would be the limiting case for Kepler's third law, so regardless of whether any physical planet could actually exist there, what orbital velocity corresponds to this distance from the center of the Sun? (Please don't write in and say I forgot Venus in the diagram. I'm picking and choosing.)

Figure 15

The diameter of the Sun is 865,000 miles. It's circumference comes to nearly 2,730,000 miles. (Well, hey, Dawg! Here's a new 273!) Just as we did for Mars and Mercury, we plug these numbers into our formula, and the result is 273 miles per second for the orbital velocity of the distance from the center to the surface of the Sun—*another* new 273.

Kepler's third law holds for *any* distance from the Sun; an actual planet doesn't have to be at that distance for the law to hold true. We chose to consider the distance that corresponds to the surface of the Sun as a sort of limiting case. This distance corresponds to an orbital velocity of 273 miles per second. We have our old friend 273 twice more, once in the circumference of the Sun and the other the planetary orbital speed at its surface. Note, though, that unlike its previous occurrences, this time the numbers depend on a special unit of miles to come out right. Kilometers, say, won't work We'll come back to this.

We're not quite done. Let's find the orbital period of this hypothetical object at the surface of the Sun. The period is just the circumference divided by the velocity, which comes to an even 10,000 seconds (about 2 hours and 47 minutes), once around.

What links—nay, constrains—the Earth's orbit to the velocity of light? Where do all these powers of 10 come from? And why are there two more 273s?

Orbit of Light

Let's go back to Earth's orbit around the Sun in relation to the speed of light. What are we to make of these facts? Assuming that we can take these observations as describing the real Earth, Sun and speed of light, what have we got?

First, the particulars of Earth's orbit—its distance from the Sun and its orbital period—are related to the velocity of light by nearly exact factors of

How could this be?

1,000 and 10,000. There is only one place in the Solar System where the orbital velocity given by Kepler's third law is one ten-thousandth the velocity of light, and that is exactly where Earth is located. Next, there is only one orbital location where light takes 1,000 seconds to cross its diameter; again this is where Earth is located. These two facts are remarkable enough by themselves, but how could they both be true at the same time? How could Earth's mere distance from the Sun relate so evenly to the speed of light?

A distance of 93 million miles more or less corresponds to a Kepler orbital velocity of 18.6 miles per second; this is a well-known fact. Perhaps it is merely a coincidence that ten thousand times this is the velocity of light. But this same distance gives an orbital diameter of 186 million miles, which means it takes light 1,000 seconds to cross it. Now, we have two coincidences that relate Earth's orbital factors to the speed of light, and together they are much harder to dismiss.

There is no reason, at least on the surface of things, why these two observations should be so well-correlated with the speed of light. At 93 million miles, the orbital velocity could have been anything, say 14.5 miles per second. The orbital diameter would still correlate with the speed of light, but the orbital velocity would not. Or, suppose the orbital velocity remained 18.6 miles per second, but the orbital distance was 106 million miles. Then the velocity would still relate to the speed of light, but the orbital diameter would not.

Yet, neither of these is the case. Our Solar System is so constructed that one single orbital velocity and diameter both relate to the speed of light by even factors of 10,000 and 1,000 at the same time. And Earth is situated at the only place in the Solar System where this fact holds true. It is hard to point out too strongly how unlikely this situation is. It is not enough that the sizes of the Earth, Moon and Sun are related in the ways we have described. Nor is it enough that they are so arranged that the Moon and Sun appear to be the same size as seen from Earth. Now we find that the speed of light, one of the fundamental constants of the universe, is implicated in two interlocking ways with Earth's orbit.

This is a subtle point, but do you see the issue? First, the units of distance don't matter; kilometers work just as well as miles, because when we divide, the factors 1,000 and 10,000 have no units. More importantly, the real problem is that an orbital velocity of 18.6 miles per second corresponds to an orbital diameter of 186 million miles. The issue is only in the mind of the perceiver of these facts, not somewhere in the cold reaches of space. The issue is one of ontology, not of physics. Earth and Sun exist as physical objects on one level of reality, but these orbital numbers exist on a different level of reality, a conceptual one. It is this level where the pattern of similar numbers appears unexpectedly. In information theory, an unexpected fact is new information. It is *meaning*. This applies to all the .273 and 3.66 patterns as well. Our task here is to discover what this new information means, and then apply what we discover back into the physical world and to our own behavior if that seems warranted. At least we should find out if there is something here we should heed or can simply ignore.

Moon Nodes

Now that we've run into the speed of light, we can turn back to the Moon for a moment where we will find it again in a surprising place. Of course the Moon reflects the Sun's light to Earth, but the speed of light itself is numerically part of the Moon's motion. To wit:

The Moon's orbit is tilted with respect to the Earth's orbit by nearly 7°. This means the Moon is sometimes above and sometimes below the Earth's orbital plane. This is why solar eclipses are a rare event. Only when the Moon and Earth are in nearly the same plane with the Sun is an eclipse possible. There are two places, therefore, where the moon crosses the Earth's orbital plane, and they are on opposite sides of the Moon's orbit. These points are called the nodes of the Moon's orbit. The Moon passes through its ascending node as it passes above the Earth's orbital plane, and it passes through the descending node as it drops below this plane.

The imaginary line through these two nodes is called—wait for it—the line of nodes. The direction in space of the ascending node is called its longitude. The direction (the longitude) of this line is not fixed in space, due to the Moon's complicated motion. Instead it rotates slowly around the plane of the Earth's orbit. A full rotation takes 18.6 years.

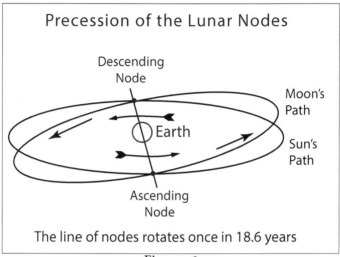

Precession of the Lunar Nodes

Descending
Node

Moon's
Path

Earth

Sun's
Path

Ascending
Node

The line of nodes rotates once in 18.6 years

Figure 16

I know. But look it up. The same digits appear in the speed of light in miles per second and in the Earth's orbital velocity in miles per second. We have already tied the speed of light with Earth's orbital speed and orbital diameter; now we are tying it to the movement of the longitude of the Moon's ascending node. We have every reason to take the length of one Earth year as a natural unit, but it is disconcerting to find this same unit expressing the speed of light (and only in miles, for some reason) again in the movement of the Moon.

Time Out for a Sec!

When I give this talk in front of a group, there is some point—usually long before now, when people begin saying, "No way." Or they shake their heads. Or gasp. One by one, though, a light goes on and they suddenly get it. One or two of these facts might be coincidental. Maybe three. But all of them? Only the most hardcore astrophysicists of a materialistic bent can continue to insist there is no pattern in the construction blueprints of the Solar System by ignoring the data and the implications of that data. Most everybody else has a slightly easier time with it.

We are going to bravely press on here. Keep in mind that a pattern means there's nothing in all this that happened by chance. Somebody or something made all these things match with the same numbers and the same ratios: 3.66, .273, 18.6.

Somebody *constructed* major parts of our Solar System in ways that we would discover sooner or later.

But it gets much, much worse.

Take a Ride on the Reading

Our Sun is among the brightest 9% of all stars in the Orion arm of the Milky Way galaxy. This makes it fairly unusual as stars go,[2] but what we want to note here is that it lies approximately 26,000 light years from the galactic center. This means that light, going at 186,300 miles per second, takes 26,000 years to get to Earth from this center. Since the galaxy is a fairly flat disc of millions of stars, there is much interstellar dust and ionized gas that obscure the center, at least for optical telescopes. So it's a difficult measurement to make, and 26,000 light years is an estimate. It could easily be 27,320 light years, but we won't push this possibility.

There is another, much closer measurement that is also nearly 26,000

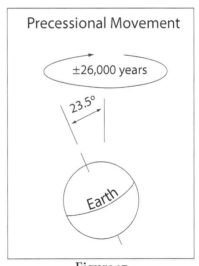

Figure 17

years long, and that is the precessional cycle of Earth's poles. It is also called the Great Year or the Platonic Year, and it means the following. If you have ever spun a top or a gyroscope you will have noticed that it doesn't spin standing upright; its upper end wobbles around in a small circle. This is called precession. The Earth is also a gyroscope in that it also spins on its axis and has a circular wobble period of about 26,000 years. This number is not known with any certainty either. It is hard to measure and appears to be changing by very small amounts in a century. This number could also easily be 27,320 years, but this is not what is so interesting about these two numbers: a distance of 26,000± light years and an Earth-related precessional time span of 26,000± years. Is there any other reason to believe these measurements are connected? There is.

If you draw an imaginary line from the Sun to the galactic center, the orbital path of Earth just happens to intersect this line. There is no obvious reason why this should be so; perhaps it's just by chance, since Earth and the other planets could have any other orientation to the galactic center. It may not be by chance, though.[3]

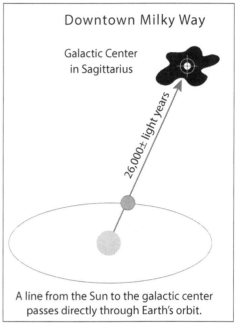

A line from the Sun to the galactic center passes directly through Earth's orbit.

Figure 18

It is another bit of circumstantial evidence that connects Earth with its greater environment, which this time is not the nearby Moon and Sun, but the far greater distance to the center of the Milky Way. (For comparison, light takes 8+ minutes to arrive from the Sun; it takes 26,000 years to arrive from downtown galaxy central.) Note that the plane of Earth's orbit doesn't coincide with the plane of the galaxy; it is tilted by about 60°. In the night sky, the galactic center is in the direction of the constellation Sagittarius.

It is not possible to conclude what meaning this numerical match-up might have, lacking any additional data. (For the same reason, it's not possible to conclude there's no connection, either.) There doesn't appear to be anything special about a 26,000 light year distance. No one knows why the Earth precesses at a 26,000 year rate. The numbers are the same, though, and they are very close to our canonical number 27.3 times 1,000. In passing, also note the following embedded assumption: Just because Earth's poles precess with a 26,000 year period doesn't mean this movement has been going on that long. This is merely the rate they're precessing at the present time; we don't know when this motion started, nor do we know what started it.

137 Ways to Say Hello

Feel like a little dessert? Here's a last morsel that neatly sums up all that we've talked about so far, plus it throws all the rest of physics into this numerical conspiracy as a bonus. This little bit of sweetness is called the *fine structure constant*, a.k.a. α or *alpha* to physicists. It's defined by the seemingly simple expression

$$\alpha = e^2\ /\ \hbar c \approx 1/137$$

As you can see, its equal to about 1/137. (More precisely it's 1/137.036... The squiggly lines mean about equal to.) This expression appears in one of the formulas in quantum physics, but since we're not doing that here, we can flip it over and just talk about 137. The Nobel prize-winning physicist Richard Feynman, the story goes, suggested that all physicists make a sign that said "137" and

The fine structure constant

hang it on their office wall to remind them how much about physics was still unknown. Another Nobel prize winner, Leon Lederman, has this to say:

> This number is related to the probability that an electron will emit or absorb a photon. [This] one number, 137, contains the crux of electro-magnetism (the electron), relativity (the velocity of light), and quantum theory (Planck's constant) . [...]
>
> The most remarkable thing about this remarkable number is that it is dimension-free. [It] turns out that when you combine the quantities that make up alpha, all the units cancel! [This] means that scientists on Mars, or on the fourteenth planet of the star Sirius, using whatever god-awful units they have for charge, speed, and their version of Planck's constant, will also get 137. It is a pure number.
>
> Physicists have agonized over 137 for the past eighty years. Werner Heisenberg once proclaimed that all the quandaries of quantum mechanics would shrivel up when 137 was finally explained.[4]

As early as the 1920s physicists began referring to 137 as a "mystical number." Arnold Sommerfeld discovered this number in 1915, or rather its reciprocal, the plain decimal number .00729. Soon, though, it was referred to as 137, which Wolfgang Pauli—another of the main architects of quantum theory—believed to be so fundamental it should be deducible from elementary particle theory. So far, however, no one has been able to do this.

A few comments are in order to understand this *alpha*, the fine structure constant, a little better before we see how it fits in with the rest of our evidence. (The fit is pretty easy to find; think about it while reading through this brief digression.) First, what does Lederman mean by "dimension-free"? It means *alpha* has no units, like inches or seconds. If, by example, we think of a rectangle that's 2 times as wide as it is high, the number 2 has no units; it's just 2—twice as wide as high. And it's always going to be two for this rectangle, whether we measure the sides in inches or centimeters or anything else. Another example is $\pi = 3.1416...$ which is the ratio of the circumference of a circle to its diameter; again it doesn't have any units. Our number 0.2732 is another example when it refers to a square and an inscribed circle. These are natural, universal constants, and so is *alpha*, the fine structure constant.

By the way, the term "fine structure" refers to a feature of atomic spectra to which *alpha* is related—no, I didn't think you wanted to know any more about it, and it isn't necessary to understand any more for our purposes here, other than to note it's a real, observable phenomenon.

Now about those letters that comprise *alpha*. This is necessarily going to be a simplified explanation, but don't think for a New York minute that a deeper, more professional exposition of these topics would clear anything up that might feel a bit hazy to you at this point. We've all heard the terms "electron," "light," "electrical charge" and so forth, but nobody—not even the Nobel prize winners—really know what they mean. That said, here are the accepted descriptions.

The electric charge on an electron is denoted by *e*. The electron is an elementary particle (along with the proton and neutron) that comprise atoms. (Well, the electron is thought to be quark-y by some, but we're ignoring that here.) All electrons (are thought to) have the same amount of charge, and no lesser or greater amount of charge has ever been observed. But *alpha* contains two *e*'s multiplied together, and if you remember that unlike charges attract and like charges

e is the electric charge on an electron

repel, e^2 is the strength with which two electrons interact. Note that no one has ever or will ever see an electron, but its properties can be inferred by experiment, sometimes quite accurately, as we'll see next.

The fundamental quantity of quantum mechanics is called Planck's constant, h, named after the first-rank German physicist Max Planck who first proposed it just at the turn of the nineteenth century. This appears in the formula for *alpha* as $\hbar$ which is pronounced "h-bar." It's equal to $h / 2\pi$ which is often how the former quantity is written in equations. Yes, that's

h is Planck's Constant

great, you say, but what does it mean? Since h (or $\hbar$) appears in dozens of places in quantum theory, a complete description isn't possible here, but one of its earliest and most important uses is easy to understand. (Well, nobody actually *understands* it, but it's easy to get a picture that probably corresponds to reality in some way.)

Suppose you're an electron, just hanging around inside an ordinary hydrogen atom. It's a pretty quiet day, and you feel listless and have little energy. Your buddy the proton (the other part of the hydrogen atom) is a pretty steady fellow, off somewhere nearby, but you, you rascal, are pretty restless all the time, and nobody ever knows where you are inside the atom. Sometimes you're over here, sometimes over there, sometimes on top, sometimes behind the proton. Nobody ever knows exactly where you are, you little imp. But listless as you are at the moment, all this flitting around the proton is your natural state; you can't help it.

But now, something wild and shocking happens: you get hit by a passing photon! Photons are what we think the smallest bits of electromagnetic energy are composed of. This particular photon is a tiny bit of light. It smacks you right in the chest, but instead of bouncing off right away, it goes inside you and Sally watch out!! Now you've got energy in spades! Kiss that proton goodbye. You've jumped away and are flying higher than ever—you're in orbit, baby! (Well, in a higher orbit, as it were, as if there actually were

Electron meets wild and crazy photon—goes nuts.

orbits. We can't get too literal here.) But this energy-level can't last or you'll go nuts, so all of a sudden you regurgitate all that energy back out in one gigantic barf and the photon leaves with its energy as quickly as it arrived. The original, "Wham, bam, thank you, Ma'am."

The essence of quantum mechanics is captured in its name; "quantum" is associated with the concept "quantized," which means little chunks. The concept is exactly like the coins you find in every currency; there's always a smallest coin. A dollar, for example, is divided into 100 pennies. You can't have 1/3 of a penny. Similarly, in quantum physics, energy doesn't just come in any old sizes. Energy chunks are characterized by a number (a very small number) which is Planck's constant, h. So our electron didn't just gradually rise to a new energy level as we might imagine a high jumper or pole vaulter would, but instantaneously jumped from a low energy to a higher one without going through any intermediate levels. It's like the fast way to eat a meatball: instead of cutting it in smaller pieces first, you just cram it into your mouth all at once, getting the spaghetti sauce all over your … (Did you get the picture with that last one?)

In an atom, there are many different discrete energy levels an electron can have, and many ways it can jump among them. But it is never seen taking shortcuts or only going halfway; the level restrictions Planck's constant imposes are always obeyed. And just to tidy up, it is incorrect to imagine the electron is any kind of ball in orbit around the atom's nucleus. The electron can be imagined as being somewhere inside a "cloud" that encloses the nucleus; that's what all the indeterminate flitting about was meant to illustrate. The incoming photon isn't a hard or solid bit of anything either. It's some kind of tiny spread-out disturbance that always travels at the same speed (we think, but maybe not always), and we call this speed the speed of light (I just had to say it right out, even though you already knew), and denote this speed by c, which is the third letter in our formula.

c is the speed of light

So there it is. Each of these constants have complicated units (c is the simplest, [distance]/[time]), but when combined as in the formula above, all the units cancel and the result is very close to 137. The real question is why 137 and not 42 (like Douglas Adams fancied in *Hitchhiker's Guide to the Universe)*, or some other number? Nobody knows. But there *is* this, which is the punch line.

I looked at *alpha* and Planck's constant and G, the gravitational constant, for a long time, and didn't see any way to connect any of them to the other pattern numbers we've discovered in our exploration of the Solar System. But then I myself got struck by some stray photons or something, and suddenly I saw how it fit. (Did you see it also?)

Twice 137 is 274.

Now this is pretty close to our 273, but is it close enough for a cigar? I decided to see how far off it was, which you do, again, by taking the difference between the two values and dividing by the desired value, and expressing the result as a percentage. So 274 - 273 divided by 273 is .366%. Here are our old friends 273 and 366 in an encore appearance. Except this time they aren't confined or centered in our corner of the Solar System, or even between here and the galactic center. The fine

Close enough for a cigar?

structure constant is, we think, an attribute of the entire universe. The reason for the factor of 2 between 137 and 274 remains to be explained. Is something divided in two parts? Do two things have to be reunited in some way? It turns out this is exactly right, but we will defer the explanation until the very end of our inquiry.

So we'll leave it there for the numbers and the patterns among them. They are all summarized in the Appendix. Now, we need to ask this: Why should the universe—near and far—reflect humans and our place here on Earth so accurately and repetitively? What do these patterns mean? We'll take up these questions after we look critically at what we discovered, and address some likely objections to it.

3

The Arguments

I Object!

We have looked at lots of data, and pointed out some startling implications, but some people will take exception to this whole affair. So before addressing the real implications of our data, let's reply to a few objections that may have arisen.

1. It's still all a coincidence.

Objection: "Granted, the number 273 comes up over and over, which may not be coincidence. But, the fact that even multiples of orbital velocity and distance correspond evenly to the velocity of light mean nothing. There is no principle known to modern physics or astronomy that might explain such correlations. Therefore, this is just much ado about nothing."

Reply: It is true that no known principle explains these facts, but that is no justification to ignore them. It is just the pursuit of such an unknown cause or principle that interests us. It is a common, but incorrect, procedure to argue from known principles that new facts and conclusions about them are either true or untrue. Instead, one must try to explain new data by using the principles and "laws" one has. If this does not work, if no explanation can be found, then either new principles must be found, old ones must be discarded, or both. In this case, since there seem to be no existing known principles, we must look for new ones, without any initial regard for how well or ill they might fit with what we think we know at the present time. In the long view of the

New principles of physics must be found

history of science, there has never been a time when scientific "laws" could explain all observations and data, and there is no reason to suspect we have reached such a point now. Nor has there ever been a time when these so-called "laws" were correct and complete, so there is no reason to suspect they are correct now. Quite the contrary, physics, and especially astronomy, are in such disarray at the present time that many in these fields are looking for new understandings to replace existing theories that no longer match observational data. In that spirit, we will carry on to other possibilities.

2. A favored choice of units fudges the data.

OBJECTION: "You used English miles in some of your relationships. Perhaps if you had used kilometers as the astronomers do, the numerical ratios would be different. Miles are not a favored unit of length in the Solar System."

REPLY: For the Earth, Sun and speed of light, the units don't matter. If we used kilometers, we would also have had to use the numerical speed of light in kilometers—299,800 km/sec—and all the numerical ratios would have been the same. The units cancel and we are left with pure numbers.

We did find, however, that the speed of a planet at the surface of the Sun is 273 miles per second and the Sun's circumference is 2,730,000 miles. It is true that only statute miles and modern seconds of time gives this result. For this number to be significant, miles would have to be some kind of favored unit of length, as would seconds as units of time.

English miles seem to be a favored unit of length in the solar system

This is the same issue as the temperature of absolute zero. In Celsius or Centigrade units, it is -273.2 degrees, but in Fahrenheit units, it is -459 degrees. Again, 273 miles per second is equivalent to 439 kilometers per second, a number that doesn't fit.

Are miles somehow a favored unit just because 2-7-3 seems to be a favored number? For a temperature scale, we had water as a justifiable reference as was noted. Is there a way we can also justify miles? There is.

We will start with the constant 0.273 we derived in our examination of a circle inscribed inside a square, which is a dimensionless number and, as a fundamental number, doesn't depend on any astronomical measurement. We found that the circumference of the Sun is very close to 2,730,000 miles. Since this is a multiple of our new natural constant, .273, the mile must in some way also be a natural constant, or very close to one.

Now the logical next step might be to look at the Earth and try to find some echo of the mile embedded in some measurement, such as the polar diameter or equatorial circumference. This can indeed be done (as, for example, Knight and Butler did in *Civilization One*[5]), but we need not get bogged down here in ancient units and conversion factors. Instead, we shall appeal circumstantially to the simple numbers cited above: the diameters of the Earth, Moon, and Sun are all multiples of simple integers :

There's a pattern here ...

- 8 x 9 x 10 x 11 is the Earth's diameter in miles.

- 8 x 9 x 10 x 3 is the Moon's diameter in miles.

- 8 x 9 x 10 x 12 is 1/100 of the Sun's diameter in miles, within less than half a percent. 100 is just a scaling factor.

From these products we can see that starting from a definition of a mile in terms of some Earth unit wouldn't by itself be enough to indicate a real pattern; we would then have to somehow also relate the mile to the Moon and Sun. But here the job is already done. The mile is already a canonical unit, precisely because it relates Earth-Moon-Sun in this simple, integral way.

The word "canonical" means characteristic of a basic pattern or form. It also means something that is recognized or accepted by virtue of its appearance in such patterns or forms. We have several objects—Sun, Earth, Moon and the relationships among them—that display easily-seen numerical patterns in miles; therefore, we are justified in recognizing and accepting English miles as a basic and natural canonical unit to describe them. The very existence of these patterns makes miles a canonical unit of the objects they describe.

In addition, as John Michell first pointed out[6], $12^5/10$ or 24,883.2 miles is the mean circumference of Earth to an accuracy of 99.99%. More small integers and powers thereof, which constitute another pattern of concise elegance physicists are so fond of. Looks like miles really are a favored unit. The mile, in terms of the dimensions of our neighborhood of the Solar System, is therefore a fundamental unit, or perhaps a fraction of a larger fundamental unit or a multiple of a smaller one. Either way, it is clearly also a natural unit (since it occurs in nature), so we will accept it as such.

Why should $12^5/10$ be Earth's circumference in miles?

How about the second? Is it a natural unit or just an arbitrary duration? Since one Earth day is clearly a natural unit, integral multiples or fractions of it are also natural units. And it doesn't matter which day we take, the mean solar day of 86,400 seconds or the sidereal day of 86,164 seconds; small differences only appear in the third significant place.

This dispenses with the favored units question. All the numbers we have used consist either of units that cancel or of natural units. The fact that modern physics does not currently use all these natural units in no way disqualifies them.

3. Close, but no cigar

OBJECTION: "A lot of your numbers are close to real physical constants, but you've just cherry-picked specific numbers from a range and used that to justify your fore-ordained conclusion. For example, the Earth's orbital diameter is indeed 186,300 miles at certain times in its orbit, but it also has different values that occur just as often in a year. The same holds for Earth's orbital speed: it isn't always 18.6 miles per second; it has a range of values. You'd better stick to hard physics and forget all the speculation about a message."

REPLY: We are not trying to do hard physics; we are looking for patterns in numbers taken from the observed Solar System and our local environment, that are not the *exclusive* domain of astronomy and physics. We've found many patterns that are so improbable that they can't possibly all be coincidences.

The point of this exercise is not to do physics, astronomy or biology, but to use the results of these sciences to bring into focus a giant billboard with a very surprising message, one that exists despite the current state of understanding in these disciplines. We are saying the purview of these sciences isn't nearly broad and deep enough to adequately explain their own data; big chunks of understanding are missing

Have we been missing something?

that are extraordinarily important for us as human beings to comprehend. So by using astronomical data we can make a point that's contained in that data; we can draw conclusions that have so far been missed, at least in modern times.

Now regarding the number ranges in some of our examples. Our world is in a constant state of change, of becoming. Nothing stays the same; there is always movement and variation. Constant, dynamic movement means measurements will always change. Things don't hold still for a spot-on value and they never will. That's the point, and that's the nature of reality on both ends of our telescopes. Nothing will be exact or constant; remember, the so-called physical "constants" are really a statistical averaging of a great many different measurements. There is even speculation among some scientists that physical constants themselves aren't really constant over long periods of times or in different places. (This is actually a hot topic among post-grad school foundational physicists. Geezer physicists.)

Instead of looking at a range of values and thinking that the desired number is merely one of them, consider instead that a range of observed values clusters around one special, favored value as a result of constant movement and change. If you cut a circle out of a piece of paper with a scissors that is supposed to be four inches in diameter, then repeat the same thing many more times, your paper circles will all have slightly different diameters, which will all cluster around four inches, but will all be off by some small amount. Try the experiment in a pick-up truck driving down a bumpy dirt road and your circles (if they're still even circles) will have a much wider size variation. If you cut out enough of them, though, you can still tell they cluster around four inches. What is special about four inches? If you gave your stack of paper circles to someone else, could they deduce that you tried to make them all exactly four inches across? Possibly not, especially if they didn't use inches as a unit. But if you started by trying to cut out two different sizes of paper circles that were, say, 2 inches and 6.3 inches across, they would be more likely to say, "Hey, if I divide the sizes of your larger circles by your smaller ones, I get numbers that are pretty close to *pi*. I bet that's what you were trying to show me." This is exactly what we've done here. "Hey, Earth's orbital diameter is pretty close to the digits in the speed of light, and so is its orbital speed. How could that be?"

To find a pattern is to find meaning

To find a pattern is to find meaning. If you look under a rock and find a penny, you might think perhaps somebody was walking along, dropped or threw away the penny, heavy rain fell sometime later and washed that penny near a rock that happened to tip over on top of it in the torrent of water that ran by from the rain. You might think no more about it. But if you turned over six other rocks and they also had pennies under them, you would be justified in thinking, "Hey, somebody's been putting pennies under all these rocks! Why would they do that?" Why indeed?

To anticipate another possible objection, we present a note from one of our sponsors, the Mathematics Department. It seems these days the longer the string of digits you have, the more impressive your results will be. If you cite π as 3.14159265 you're an expert. If you use 3.14 you're a piker. A mere hacker. Yet if you're a metal smith who needs to cut a bar of wrought iron to form a two foot circle, 3.14 will do just fine. A more serious problem has to do with significant digits, which you might recall from high school. If a crucial piece of your data has only three significant digits, you are not allowed to cite a result after some calculations that has eight significant digits no matter how good your arithmetic is. Your results can have no more accuracy than your input. So we are happy here with three significant digits, sometimes four when the data warrants, because these are enough to show the pattern that emerges on its own.

However, there is something else, more fundamental, regarding *number* as a principle of manifestation in relation to the measurement of actual objects. Earlier, we wondered if the dimensions of a physical object, such as the Earth, wasn't the effect of a more primal cause. This was one of Plato's primary tenants, that there exists an archetypal, primal plane of reality, consisting of patterns, of which our physical reality is just a reflection, subject to the fluctuations of vibration, movement and motion that is characteristic of it. This view was expressed, for example, by Nicohachus of Gerasa in the first or second century CE. These patterns, he says

> were fixed, like a preliminary sketch, by the domination of number pre-existent in the mind of the world-creating God, number conceptual only and immaterial in every way, but at the same time the true and eternal essence, so that with reference to it, as to an artist's plan, should be created all these things: time, motions, the heavens, the stars, and all kinds of revolutions … [Number] existed before everything else in the mind of the creating God, like some universal and exemplary plan, relying upon which as a design and archetypal example the Creator of the universe sets in order his material creations and makes them attend to their proper ends.[7]

Leaving aside his identification of the creative agency as "God" for the moment, he is expressing the idea that the dimensions of Earth as a principle, archetype or pattern, came before the physical Earth which is merely an instantiation or reflection of it. Since the reflecting medium—our space and time—is not perfect, the reflection is not perfect either. The very process from pattern to instance introduces noise, as it were. Here's an example. The Earth has an equatorial diameter of 7927 miles, a polar radius of 7901 miles and a mean (average) radius of 7918 miles.

Numeric patterns are archetypes

These differing values—which appear as noise, the effects of moving in space and time—do not prevent us from using 7920 miles as the canonical or archetypal value *precisely because* the numerical relations work out for it. For to insist that 7918 miles, for example, should be used, is to deny the ontological existence of an archetypal realm of which 7918 is just an approximation. Indeed, this whole exercise is to demonstrate that there is, in fact, such a primal realm behind the physical one we apprehend with our senses and instruments, so as to ask not only why there are such reflections, but what our purpose might be among them? Then we wish to step to the ultimate questions: Are we ourselves also such reflections, and, if so—and not being content to be a mere reflection—how do we get to the essential, archetypal level of our own beings? How do we contact the true reality behind the reflection?

All genuine spiritual traditions (of which the world's religions are *their* imperfect reflections) have addressed this question. The Tantric scriptures, for example, call the physical world of reflections *maya* or illusion—something not quite real. More precisely, something

Okay. Here's the illusory part.

incompletely real. Fabricated. This means there is a part of reality beyond the physical universe that we apprehend with our ordinary senses. What immediately concerns us is that there is a message embedded in certain of these planetary and solar reflections that seems to be saying that not only are the things we ordinarily apprehend reflections of something more basic, they are also less complete—something is missing. This implies that we ourselves are incomplete, not only because we are "inside" and part of the aggregate Earth-Moon-water-Sun system, but also because it is we who apprehend it, not as outside observers, but as intrinsic components of it. Therefore we are implicated in its unreality, its incompleteness. We're fake, too.

None of this is to suggest any kind of dualism, however. The canonical, archetypal or ideal realms are embedded in the material realm, just as the canonical value of 18.6 miles per second for Earth's orbital speed is embedded in the actual range of 18.20 to 18.82. The canonical gets smeared, spread out, over a range of values due to physical movement and vibration which occur at any temperature above absolute zero. The apparent separation of ontological realms is perceptual ony—a current limitation on our part.

Of course, all this is a hot topic today, although it's not stated from the point of view of numerical congruence. We'll look at a bit of this argument below, but first one final question all the "nothing-but" reductionists are jumping up and down about.

4. Parts is parts

OBJECTION: "Sure, these numbers and concepts have the relations among them you've pointed out, but they aren't real, because none of these relations are physically overt, like poodles or asteroids. They're just abstract concepts, nothing more."

REPLY: We must be sure we understand exactly where these numbers and concepts constellate themselves, for the answer will lead to the solution of their very mystery. So where do they exist? Not out "there" in the physical universe, where they don't overtly appear; after all, they're just a collection of seemingly disparate measurements and observations. A few numbers and ratios. So in that real sense, they're not "physical" at all. (For the moment, we will avoid the larger question, "Is anything physical?" but we'll get back to it below.) Meanwhile, we note that they only display the concealed meanings we've uncovered in the mental realm where they form an interlocking and self-referential web or pattern of meanings that is separate from the physical realm.

In fact, it is hard—impossible, actually—to see how this web of meanings could have derived from their physical referents, which is demonstrated by the very disparate nature they display; pregnant mothers, after all, have no physical relation to physics experiments near absolute zero, say (at least one hopes they don't!), or to the size ratio between Moon and Earth.

The physical world derives from these archetypal patterns

But, since this web of meanings does exist, the relationship between the physical and mental realms must be the other way around: All the relationships we have been discussing must be causally senior and prior to the physical universe, which is but an instantiation of them.

Put differently, this latter realm is not merely derivative of the physical laws we have discovered about it, but is also derivative of a set of anthropocentric, conceptual and non-physical meanings that have smeared out into a space-and-time universe that is also self-referential and interlocking, but one where the original web of meanings only exists in a differentiated form, much like the curves of a quadratic equation degenerate—disappear—upon mathematical differentiation. Only the "integration" by a conscious, human mind can make the higher-order "curves" of meaning reappear.

As for what is "real" and what isn't, our numerical and related evidence allows us to jump to the very end of the argument between the idealists and realists. At the end of our analysis we'll find there's nothing real except the Cheshire Cat's smile of awareness. Until then, it's worthwhile trotting out this old limerick:

> On campus, a student said, "God—
> I find it exceedingly odd,
> That this tree, as a tree,
> Simply ceases to be
> When there's no one about in the quad."

The Mini-Anthropic Principle

If the numbers and relationships we have found aren't coincidental, and if they're not the consequence of specially-selected units, then what do they mean? Why are they important? Scientists have considered how it can be that the universe is observable by us, and what the necessary conditions were for us to have evolved to be able to observe it at all. It's called the Anthropic Principle. In 1986 two cosmologists made the following argument: our position in the universe, while not special or central in every way, as the early Church thought, is special and central in *some* ways. The very fact that we are observers of the universe implies at least that we and it are of such a nature that we can observe it at all. In other words, the nature of the universe as we observe it—its size, age and laws of change—must be such that that we can observe these features and processes. Furthermore, the processes of the evolution of life must be such that we could and did evolve into such observers.

In their Introduction, authors Barrow and Tipler have this to say about various observations of the universe in their book *The Anthropic Cosmological Principle*:

[Any] observed properties of the Universe that may initially appear astonishingly improbable, can only be seen in their true perspective after we have accounted for the fact that certain properties of the Universe are necessary prerequisites for the evolution and existence of any observers at all. ... our own existence acts as a selection effect when assessing observed properties of the Universe.[8]

How can we be here?

A simple example of the Anthropic Principle is that the universe must be old enough for we humans to have evolved to the point where we can observe it. (Later we will see that this assumption and others like contain a conceptual error. For now, though, we'll let it stand.) Also, conditions must be met which allow carbon-based life forms like ourselves to have evolved here on Earth in the first place. But there are many other aspects of this principle, such as the necessity for the physical constants of nature to have the values they do. Why, for example, does the speed of light, c, have the value it does? Even slight changes to many of these constants would disallow life as we know it. We, as human life on Earth, must therefore have some special or favored position in the universe for us to exist at all as we do, even if there exist other parts of the universe, possibly unobservable parts, that do not have such conditions. The universe, or our corner of it at least, must somehow be fine-tuned, as it were, so that we would eventually be able to observe it. Caution must be observed here, so as not to extrapolate very scanty information into sweeping generalizations. For example, even though there are millions of other stars just like our Sun, we can draw no conclusions about any other star having an Earth-like planet, nor about the existence of life on such a planet. The problem

Our fine-tuned universe: How did it get this way?

is that we have only one data point to start with—Earth. We will never know the probability that other Earth-like planets have intelligent life just because ours does. (We are far from knowing if any of the exo-planets discovered so far have or can have our kind of life. All we know about them is their orbital periods and ballpark mass estimates.)

But we are not concerned here with such grand questions about the origin of the universe as a whole, or about whether intelligent life exists on other planets. (Indeed, some people wonder if intelligent life exists on our planet!) What we are concerned with is the possible import of so many occurrences of similar numbers in our Solar System, and how the Solar System came to exhibit them. We may take the Earth's position in the Solar System as an example. The Sun emits radiation of such a magnitude that it creates and sustains a certain temperature here on Earth that has allowed life to evolve as it has. Were the Earth farther from or closer to the Sun, it would be too cold or hot to allow our forms of life to develop. For example, at some point farther out, surface water would freeze, and at some point farther in water would boil away. As in the story of "Goldilocks and the Three Bears," Baby Bear's porridge was "just right." On Earth, liquid water is just right. We don't know for certain if life *has* to have liquid water to support it, because Earth is the only observably life-supporting planet around and that's that.

However, there *are* plenty of other moons and planets around, so it's valid to ask if any of them exhibit similar numerical factors as Earth does. They do not; the relationships among Earth, Moon and Sun are unique in the Solar System. That being the case, how did these things come about? Although it is anathema to most mainstream scientists, the Anthropic Principle in some form must be true. And on the local scale, perhaps it is not stated strongly enough.

A more recent work is *The Privileged Planet* by Gonzalez and Richards, and these authors carry the argument much farther than Barrow and Tipler did. The first part of their book examines the physical environment of the Earth and our Solar System to make the point that far from being randomly developed, we live in a highly favorable and favored corner of the galaxy. They point out, for example, that "the Sun is among the 9 percent most massive stars in the Milky Way Galaxy."[9] (The vast majority of stars are red and white dwarfs with only one tenth the mass of the Sun. Very massive stars are bright, but relatively rare.) Further, our Sun is much more stable in light output (and therefore total energy output) than other Sun-like stars, which prevents wild climate swings on Earth as a rule (although this doesn't rule them out). The overall impression from reading this book is that a great deal of care was taken by somebody or something to create the conditions that allow we humans to exist here on Earth. In fact they conclude from the evidence they present

Our Sun is a fairly rare critter

> ... that the universe is in fact designed. Physicist Paul Davies, for
> instance, reversed his earlier views, saying, "The impression of design

is overwhelming." And the late astrophysicist Fred Hoyle, one of the founders of the Steady State model and an intransigent atheist, admitted, "A commonsense interpretation of the facts suggests that a superintellect has monkeyed with physics, as well as chemistry and biology, and that there are no blind forces worth speaking about in nature.[10]

We will look at who or what this "superintellect" might be in a bit, but saying there is sharp discussion on this topic is a wild understatement. Arguments about the Anthropic Principle and related ideas rage in many quarters. It is front and center, for example, in the argument between creationists (the universe is the result of intelligent design) versus Neo-Darwinists (evolution is the result of random mutations and natural selection). Here, despite the appearance of all the math and numbers, we side neither with the stoic, inflexible "scientific" Darwinists, nor with the fundamentalism, intolerance and narrow-mindedness of the creationists. (Emotionally, one can sometimes hardly tell them apart.) Both are extreme positions, and there is a broad middle ground with many other possibilities. Fortunately, we don't need to wade into these waters, at least not very far, for we need not be concerned with the problematic arguments for or against "God," as that term is variously understood, or the equally problematic arguments for or against natural selection and evolution. We need only tear off a tiny corner of the paper where all this is writ and ask the following simple question:

Is it possible that some Agency—unknown to us—left us a message coded in the very structure of our planetary environment? And that this message was meant specifically for us humans in this brief epoch of time in which we find ourselves, say the last ten to fifteen thousand years? We can call this local version the Mini-Anthropic Principle. Assuming that some Agency in fact "monkeyed" with our Solar System, what might be the motive of such an Agency? It must be

> *If pattern is message, who left it?*

that for some reason or another we need such a message, and that it's very important that we receive and understand it, considering all the trouble this Agency took to engineer it—an activity we'll examine shortly. The message must be exceedingly important to the Agency and to us, whether or not we ourselves yet realize its importance. Furthermore, there must have been no easier ways to send the message, or if there were, their delivery and reception channels must have been deemed less reliable. A belt-and-suspenders kind of thing; a tell-me-three-times kind of thing.

Let's Sidebar Again

Time to stand aside and take our bearings before going further with the argument. Things have gotten much uglier for mainstream academic materialists since Barrow and Tippler. The main strike, unwittingly, has come from within their own ranks. The consequences of the tenets of quantum theory have introduced consciousness into the current operational theories of the physical world, right in through the front door. For it is now understood that the observer of certain physical experiments determines the outcomes of those experiments, that the mere act of observing an experiment changes its outcome. There are many popular accounts of quantum theory that explain this, or at least describe it.

The next step is to realize that we live in a "Goldilocks" universe, where so many physical constants have to be just so—neither too hot nor too cold, as it were—for the universe to exist at all, and, far more improbably, that we are in it and are able to observe it. Current theories of the universe, its origins and its on-going existence, remain tenable only if this central fact is ignored. Even the most die-hard materialists must have thought or felt at some point that their billiard ball explanations and their haphazard-mutation theory of evolution don't really explain anything, much less any substantial part of everything. Not really. But again, we are going much further than a "just right" universe here.

We begin to zero in on a new, central and necessary conclusion when we grant that consciousness and intention, operating outside the space-time universe that our instruments measure and our senses report, have in some way, unknown to us at present, constructed the universe for our benefit —at least the part that contains our local Solar environment. And not just some abstract benefit conceived in the remote past where causes are allowed to be nonspecific, or worse, completely unspecified.[11] The fact that English miles are a favored unit of construction with respect to the Sun, Earth and Moon, as are seconds of time, present a conundrum that will remain unsolvable as long as we only use sequential, linear cause and effect, and as long as we ignore not only our own consciousness, but also larger units of consciousness that extend up to the integrated universe itself and beyond. This thread will be explored in the sections that follow.

Note that this is not a religious argument, nor even a primarily spiritual one, as that term is currently defined in all its breadth. It begins from purely numerical analyses and doesn't ignore any of the results it finds. It is a logical argument that says if these are the facts we find, then we must search for the causes that explain them to the best of our abilities. Hmmm. Sounds like a scientific argument.

In summary, then, we are asking how did it come to be that we ourselves seem to be the center of attention of our local universe, despite the fact that it apparently came into existence far earlier than we ourselves did?

The situation is analogous to the famous EPR paradox in physics, only in reverse. There, Einstein and his buddies Podolsky and Rosen, theorized, as an objection to quantum theory, that two fundamental particles, like electrons or photons of light, that were once together, would continue to influence each other even when they have traveled far apart, a situation Einstein did not like. Since the idea violated his Special Theory of Relativity by implying travel faster than the speed of light, he called it "spooky action at a distance." The correct name is quantum entanglement, meaning the properties of the two particles remain "tangled" together forever; observing or changing a property of the first particle causes an immediate, mirror-image change in the second particle. Einstein was wrong. Many experiments have proved that entan-

Albert Einstein didn't like it ...

glement is real, and we have no explanation as to why this condition, called non-locality, is true.[12]

Here, though, we have a similar situation in reverse. On the one hand we have the Sun, Earth and Moon with one long-term evolutionary track, and on the other hand there is us, with a different, although embedded, short-term evolutionary track. The former we measure in billions of years; the latter we measure in well under a million years. They appear independent of each other, beyond the happenstance that we actually live on the surface of Earth. And yet the patterns and relationships we have examined force them together as surely as the EPR particles were together before the experiment began that separated them. Sun, planets, Moon, light, human ges-

... he called it "spooky action at a distance"

tation period, water and so on, may appear to be separate, but this is only appearance. It must be that we humans are an integral part of our environment—always have been and always will be—and that we are all causally connected, entangled, in a two-way, Tweedledee-Tweedledum sense, each pointing to the other as cause and each receiving a reflection back as effect.

We're the cause of the universe, just as much as it's the cause of us? Far out, dude.

"Kilroy was here"

Let's continue with the idea that some Agency, perhaps an abstract or even metaphorical one in some sense, is the cause or co-cause of the patterns we've been discussing. Let's deal with the question of who or what this super-intelligent Agency might be right off the bat.

- It might be "God," but that puts us squarely in the midst of an old argument that has no provable solution; besides, the term "God" has a variety of meanings that are too varied and vague to be of much help. Further, we have no evidence that this message has a God-scope. It's a message with a mostly local scope, and we are perhaps not justified in attributing to it more than local causation. Then again, it might well be universal in scope, considering the fine structure constant.

- Instead it might be some kind of agent of God, one with a more local scope, for as astronomer Sir James Jeans once remarked, "God is a mathematician." Most of the numerical patterns we've found are from our local solar environment.

- Then again, this Agency might be extra-terrestrial beings, who are often made unseen scapegoats of all sorts of things, since we don't seem capable of doing them ourselves, whether we actually are capable of doing them or not. We have no evidence for an ET cause one way or another.

- It might be ourselves, who have traveled back from the future into the far past billions of years ago, as some authors have fancied, in order to, say, rig the Moon to have the size and position it does today. Again, though, no data.

- Finally, it could be an intelligence from a different plane of existence, one with a different ontological reality, to whom we might attribute certain God-like abilities. There, perhaps planet-designing is covered in Solar System Engineering 201. This other ontological realty is where our local reality was/is engineered.

The question is fairly moot, however, as at the present time we have no way to tell who or what this Agency might be, only that there is one. (Note, though, we do not exclude the possibility that there may be ways to discover the nature of and, indeed, make contact with such an Agency. Or with the other level of reality mentioned in that last bullet point. Our last chapter concerns this very possibility.)

A more important question is what does the message mean? Specifically, what does it mean for us, since we're the ones who have apprehended it? If the numerical relationships we have covered are absurd, then perhaps the message is that the objects they describe are also absurd, meaning too improbable to be natural. We are prone to believe what we see, but not even Alice's White Queen could believe so many absurd things before breakfast. The relationship among the Earth, Sun and Moon is artificial: orbits, sizes and times of revolution and rotation. Constructed. Altered from some previous unknown configuration. All the connections that share a factor of .273 or 3.66 or 18.6, or a decimal multiple of these factors, have been engineered to have the values they do. Water, its melting and boiling points, absolute zero where all thermal motion ceases, the Moon, the human gestation period, the speed of light. All twiddled, nudged, altered to match a seemingly insignificant number that arises from the simple geometry of a square and

What does the message mean for us?

an inscribed circle: 0.2732. For good measure, Earth's orbit is directly related to the speed of light. Talk about throwing light on a subject...

The conclusion seems to be that a good part of our immediate environment in space and on Earth, too, is artificial. Not random, but somebody's hands-on. What else might be artificial, constructed with a purpose, that additional investigation might reveal? But the real punch line is this: If we are smack dab in the middle of this "stage play," and are, indeed, "on stage" ourselves, in that we are physically 70% water—water, which is deeply implicated in this whole business—then what if we too are in some sense artificial? Artificial, not in the sense of being androids or something of that kind, but of being other than merely the result of random mutations and natural selection?

All artificial constructions are made with a purpose. We are not sure if so-called "natural" objects also have a purpose, but this is not our subject. We may not know what the purpose of an artificial object is, but that's not necessary. Nor is it necessary to know how the object might have been made, altered, tweaked and so on. The form, mechanism or means of delivery of a message is separate from the content of the message. Speculation on the former is fine, as long as it doesn't detract from efforts to understand the latter.

If the Sun, Earth and Moon are even partly artificial, then they are unnatural. Also, if their relative sizes and configurations are artificial, these are also unnatural. They are therefore unreal, or at least represent only a partial reality, in the sense that their existence has a cause or causes not evident to our perception; therefore these causes must also be part of reality. If I am walking in the desert and come across a billboard, I know that it is not a real or natural part of the desert; I know that it must have been brought here and erected by someone. It is or was part of something that is not part of the natural desert.

If it's artificial, it was made by "somebody," and has a purpose.

So I have divided the desert in two parts: one part that is the natural desert—the sand, rocks, scrub brush and so on, and another part that was imported and constructed. The billboard is not part of the natural desert, it's just now physically located within the natural desert. Therefore, the world must consist of not only the desert that I see, but also consist of the makers of the billboard and *their* world as well, who I don't see on my desert walk.

By analogy, if the Moon's configuration, say, is artificial, then the universe, or at least our corner of the Solar System, consists of that which we can see with our eyes or through our telescopes, and in addition the ontological reality of an unknown Agency that created or tweaked it—a part of reality we can't see. Here, the word "ontological" means existing; having a real existence. A real *physical* existence, though, is not necessarily implied.

It doesn't matter whether this Agency is still around or not. It doesn't matter who, what, or where this Agency is. There is no data to support any conclusions. Going back to the billboard in the desert, it doesn't matter who built it, how they brought it to the desert, or where the construction crew is now. All that matters is *what the billboard says*.

So what is the message contained in the fact of a partly artificial Solar System? We have found a message that appears to come from a different, somehow more fundamental, reality which is saying,

> *What you see in your skies is an artificial construct. The Earth, Sun and Moon and their configuration did not result from purely natural causes. Our message is local; it singles you out from the rest of the universe. The naturalness you attribute to some objects isn't real. Can you be sure, therefore, that you yourselves are wholly natural? Wholly real? Get the message?*

4

THE IMPLICATIONS OF THE PATTERNS

TO RECAP: ARE we really sure there is a billboard with a message on it? Are we really sure the sizes, configurations and relations of Earth-Moon-Sun-water-humans is a sign of artificiality? The Sun-Earth-Moon system is too improbable to have evolved by itself. Not only do the sizes and relative distances of these objects strongly suggest a plan or design, the fact that the speed of light was liberally "planted" so that someone, sooner or later, would sit up and take notice cannot have been an accident either. To arrange all this the orbital mechanics of the entire Solar System must either have been adjusted at some point or have been engineered this way from the get go, which appears to be about 4.5 billion years ago, the supposed age of the Solar System.

Were this all, we might be forgiven for saying, "That's nice, but it's not really important. Those funny numbers are just up there in the sky; nothing to do with us—we've got our own problems."

... and we're all implicated

However, this is not the situation. What strikes home the strongest is the fact that ten lunar sidereal months equal the human gestation period. This moves the number 0.2732 and everything related to it inside every mother-to-be. And the fact that this same number is intrinsically related to water, which constitutes 70% of our bodies, brings it right inside everyone else. So what are the implications?

It is absurd to think all these "coincidences" are natural. Therefore, they must be artificial. Which implies that some Agency, of which we have no knowledge, engineered them. Again, we don't know how. Next, if we are embedded within this artificiality, this implies we, too, are at least partly artificial. But, despite the fact that we don't know who engineered all these things, we can ask what purpose this artificiality might have? Since we are implicated in it neck deep, the purpose must have something to do with us as a race of human beings who have become aware of it. The purpose must represent some kind of an intelligent message to us. To prepare ourselves to answer this question, we can first take a look at what kind of engineering must have been done to send the message to us in the first place. I have called this the Backstage Theory. It can help give us some insight into what it would take to send it and how important this must have been, and must still be.

Then we will be in a position to look at what the contents and meaning of this message might be. I have called this the Forgetful Partner Theory.

The Backstage Theory

This theory describes the kinds of methods that some unknown Agency would have to have used to construct not only the Solar System as we see and measure it, but also at some point have to have used to build in all the relationships and patterns we have pointed out. All this happened "backstage," out of sight, before we came along to observe it and participate in it. We have no knowledge of whether this "creation" or "construction" was done when the Solar System was formed, or much later. There is no reason to suppose it was not done as late as 10,000 years ago, a time for which we have no information about the heavens, only speculations, extrapolations, and guesses. Since we don't know how it was done, we can't speculate on when it was done. (We do wonder *why* it was done, however.) But what exactly would have to have been done to arrange the Sun, Earth and Moon as we observe them today? Plus all the other details we've gone through?

First, the geometry of space would have to be set. This is so that the value of π is determined so that our circle inscribed within a square calculation will come out to 0.2372. This is a fundamental ratio upon which all the later ratios depend, such as the Earth-Moon size ratio. Then the speed of light will have to be known so the Earth's orbital distance from the Sun can be set. This is all just preliminary groundwork. Now comes the hard part. Let's play Solar System engineering.

Solar System Engineering 201: Course description

The Earth's orbital speed must center around 18.6 miles per second so as to be a decimal fraction of the speed of light. (Did I mention that a base 10 number system must be used? This Agency had to fore-know that we observers would have ten fingers and would use them for counting.) Next, the orbital size also has to be an exact decimal fraction of the speed of light so that light would cross it in 1,000 seconds. Suppose, though, that upon the first try the orbital speed did not correlate with the orbital diameter. For the required orbital speed, the orbital size was too big or too small. They need to match, so the Agency would have to get out its toolbox. The required adjustment would be to the so-called universal gravitational constant, usually denoted as G. This constant famously appears in Newton's Law of Gravity equation, which states that the force of gravity between two bodies is the product of their masses divided by the square of the distance between them, all multiplied by this constant, G, to make the units come out right. G also figures into the proportionality constant of Kepler's third law (gory math omitted), which acts to fine-tune the equation. This means that by fiddling with G we could either draw the planets closer to the Sun or push them farther away, while their orbital speeds remained the same. Said another way, G sets the scale of the Solar System. Of course, tweaking

This was the original version of Whack-a-Mole the gravitational constant has side effects. All the planets and moons in the Solar System would be affected, as would the Milky Way and the rest of the galaxies, assuming G is universal, but what the hey. The message is for us Earthians, so no expense was spared.

Oh, wait. The Earth also has to have an orbital period just over 365 days so that it will make 366 revolutions per year. But this requirement mucks up the adjustments we just made to G, so something a little more serious will have to be tweaked. That would be *c*, the speed of light. This is because so many things have to balance just right: orbital speed (18.6 miles per second), orbital diameter (186,300 miles) and orbital period (about 365 days, one year). Also, we'll need to make sure that the orbital velocity of a hypothetical object at the Sun's surface will be 273 miles per second and have a period exactly 10,000 seconds. Back into the toolbox for more tweaking.

Earth days are not set yet, nor are miles (on Earth) or seconds. Also, we don't have the correct sizes for anything yet, so we should get on all this PDQ. We can get Earth sized correctly, then spinning on its axis, which will set days and seconds. Tilt the Earth over in its orbit by 23½° and get it precessing with a period of roughly 26,000 years to match the distance to the big shebang at the galactic center.

Miles are a problem. We've already locked miles into Earth's orbital elements and the speed of light, but how to get us Earthians to use them? Ah yes, the product of those integers (e.g. 8 x 9 x 10 x 11 was the Earth's diameter in miles). Now, when measurements are made in miles the other numerical relationships will be noticed. "Multiplying four small integers is so clever of us engineers! How dumb will those Earthians have to be not to see our little joke."

On to sizes. It's best to start with the Sun, which must have a circumference of 2,730,000 miles. We'd just better hope this gives a surface-level orbital velocity of 273 miles per second, or we'll have to putz around with G and c some more. In the worst-case scenario, which is most likely, these numbers *don't* match, so back into the toolbox. Either we can give π the old Procrustean bed treatment, making it a

A joke on us dumb Earthians ...

bit larger or smaller to fit, or we can fiddle with, say, mass. Nobody really knows what mass *is* (which is sort of a surprise, but there you are), but the Agency engineers certainly do. Possibly the electric charge will have to be diddled, or the proton's charge to mass ratio, which (long sigh) will ripple across the universe—a creator's job is never done...

... but we'll leave the rest of the details to the engineers, as you've probably got the idea by now. We haven't even considered the Moon yet, which by itself would be a piece of cake by comparison, except that it has to mesh with everything else. Then there's the water business. How are we going to get water to freeze at exactly 273.2°K and boil at 100 degrees hotter? What's more, that bun's got to stay in the oven for 273 days or know the reason why!

This is the essence of any theory of the design of our Solar System and ourselves—our whole environment, because there's a lot left out. All these little creator-details probably kept those Agency guys up late a ton of nights. But here's the thing. Now that we have a better idea of what must have been required to pull this whole thing off, the question is, is it conceiv-

The Agency guys get no sleep ...

able, even likely, that something like this really happened? Einstein said, "What really interests me is whether God had any choice in the creation of the world." This question asks if there is really only one consistent set of laws that work? Is it really possible to twiddle one or several aspects of physical reality and still have a universe that works? There can be no answer to this question because we have only this one universe—or our corner of it—as our datum. There are no others to observe, so we have no way of knowing whether any twiddling did or even could have occurred. But unless something like this scenario actually occurred, our environment—and ourselves—wouldn't have ended up like they did.

Regardless of the details of how this may have been done, it must have been extremely important to do it. Also note the scope of what was involved—it possibly extended far past the Solar System all the way to the galactic center. To *every* galactic center, considering that the fine structure constant is involved.

Mull this over. We'll come back to how this might really have happened in a bit.

False and Consequences

The Latin phrase *post hoc, ergo propter hoc* means—in case you missed that episode of *The West Wing*—"after it, therefore because of it." It describes

| The West Wing, first season, Episode 2 |

a kind of invalid logic where if B follows A, then B must have been caused by A. It is true that I am hungry because I have not eaten all day, but it is not true that there are no lions around here because I put up "Lions Keep Out" signs. Not eating for a sufficient time always produces hunger, but many reasons exist why there are no lions roaming my neighborhood. I might live in Alaska, for example. We cannot reason backwards from effects to causes without the greatest care, for it is easy to attribute false causes to any situation. What came earlier did not necessarily cause what came later.

In our context, we naturally assume that the universe was created, evolved or came about somehow prior to our emergence as an intelligent species, who are then able to observe it in all its beauty, splendor and, above all, enormous size. But is it possible that this could be a *post hoc* assumption? The universe is supposed to be at least 10 billion years old, and we puny humans have been around for only some hundreds of thousands of years—barely a tiny droplet in an ocean of time. Surely the universe, or some aspect or cause of it, brought us into being. This cause might be God or some set of natural, evolutionary, physical processes. It was all here before us, therefore he/she/it was the cause of us.

Things are not so clear, however, when we examine the assumptions embedded in this statement. We think the universe looks extremely old, because we have assigned certain time spans to its creation and development. It *must* be a certain minimum age because we think we know how long certain parts of it would take to appear as they are now, based on natural, physical laws and processes we think are correct. Some of these "laws" come from Earth-based experiments, and we have no apparent reason to think they don't work everywhere and everywhen else. Other "laws" are mathematical in nature, and they describe aspects of the physical universe, even though they don't *explain* those aspects. We don't think it matters that these "laws" aren't explanations.

First, note that a "natural" evolution is implied, but we are arguing that much of what we observe isn't natural at all, so this explanation doesn't correspond to reality. Also note that the word "think" appeared five times in that last paragraph. Each usage indicates many unstated assumptions and opinions about the universe. Physical "laws" are deductions based on these assumptions, which are then generalized under the additional assumption that it is without error to do so. Here's a simple example. Newton's first law of motion states that objects traveling in a straight line will continue to do so unless acted on by some force that changes this motion. Sounds all right. Makes sense. However, no object has ever been observed to travel in a straight line.

Ever.

Every observable object is already traveling in some kind of curved path due to an existing force acting on it—gravity or electromagnetism, for example. It is an *assumption* that if a force wasn't acting on the object, then it would travel in a straight line. The problem is, there are no examples of this "law" from which the "law" could be derived. It's another assumption. What's worse, the "law" is untestable, which makes it meaningless. Why does this matter? Because it's the explanation of why planets circle the Sun (and the foundation of much else in physics, like simple inertia and Einstein's General Theory of Relativity, which isn't so simple). Newton said the planets would go in straight lines were it not for the force of gravity, which pulls them towards the Sun away from their otherwise straight paths. But we don't—can't—know this; it's too late, since they're already circling the Sun. This was and still is a *post hoc* assumption.

Here's another one. Gravity existed before the planets did, gravity is the force we know about, therefore gravity curves planetary orbits. QED. The point here is not to do more physics, but to show how physics "does" astronomy, perhaps incorrectly. Newton formulated his first "law" by observing the planets, and deduced that gravity, which he went on to describe (but not causally explain), moves the planets. (About the cause

Even Newton didn't know why stuff falls down

of gravity he said *hypothesis non fingo*, "I formulate no hypothesis." He didn't have a clue, and was honest enough to say so.) Maybe the planets move as they do for some other reason besides gravity. Since this is the single foundational law in all of

astronomy, we may expect that much if not most of what is built on that "law" is incorrect, or is correct for the wrong reasons.

In this spirit, it is fun quoting Buckminster Fuller, who said,

> Metaphysical has been science's designation for all weightless phenomena such as thought. But science has made no experimental finding of any phenomena that can be described as a solid, or as continuous, or as a straight surface plane, or as a straight line, or as infinite anything. We are now synergetically forced to conclude that all phenomena are metaphysical; wherefore, as many have long suspected—like it or not—life is but a dream.[13]

Nearly everyone assumes that the prior existence of the universe "caused" (in any sense of this concept one cares to adopt) the eventual existence of we humans. God created humans after He/She/It created the universe, or, at least, created the Earth so we would have a place to reside. Or, in the mechanistic view, we evolved from random bits and pieces of the already-existing universe over a long period of time. Either way, the existence of humans depended on the prior existence of the universe, as described by the Backstage Theory, for example. But if we now turn our attention to just the small part of the Solar System in which we reside, we see evidence of a signal or message to us that belies either type of creation or formation. For on the one hand, if "God" created the universe, it was apparently a long time ago, long before humans came about. How then, did all these absurd

Junkyard 747's for sale cheap—if you can find one.

number correlations and patterns come about long before we did? On the other hand, if only random mutations and natural selection created these patterns, it would be like saying, as astrophysicist Fred Hoyle once quipped, that a hurricane in a junkyard

assembled a shiny Boeing 747, which is just as absurd, regardless of how long the hurricane lasted. It's just not possible to create the greater from the lesser, regardless of whether scientists currently "think" it is.

Fuggedaboudit. This maxim applies to humans, too: The greater can never arise or evolve from the lesser. Thinkaboudit.

What's the alternative? Suppose that this creative, constructive, tweaking, altering, moving Agency acted simultaneously in regard to both ourselves and our little corner of the Solar System? Suppose we were created/tweaked so as to resonate with and fit into the Earth-Moon-Sun-water patterns, while at the same time these other things were created/tweaked to resonate with us and fit our pattern? The Agency would have to be standing outside time when they created all this, including us.

Further Noodle Baking

In the movie *The Matrix*, the Oracle told Neo she was going to bake his noodle. We're going to indulge in a little of that right now ourselves. Prepare your mental ovens!

Lynne McTaggart, in her book *The Intention Experiment*[14], devotes an entire chapter to describing a series of scientific experiments that demonstrated retrocausation: an act in the present that has an effect in the past. Here's an example of one typical experiment.

Helmut Schmidt, a physicist at Lockheed Martin, created an experiment using a random event generator, REG for short. This device randomly flips between two states: on/off, left/right, or something similar. Schmidt connected his REG to an audio amplifier that would send audible clicks to the left or right side of a pair of headphones. He started the machine and tape-recorded the results, being careful that no one, including himself, heard the clicks. He then made copies of the master tape (again with no one listening) and locked them away for safekeeping. He ran the following experiment on volunteer medical students the next day. He asked the students to listen to the tape with the intention of causing more clicks to appear in their left ears than their right ears. New student tapes were recorded during the experiment.

Everybody's noodle gets baked

After the experiment was over, Schmidt analyzed all the tapes using a computer. In 20,000 trials, 55 percent of the tapes had significantly more left-side clicks than right-side clicks. Plus, the student tapes and the locked away control tapes matched perfectly. In other words, the intentions of the volunteer students were able to alter the clicks on the locked-away control tapes that were recorded a day earlier than the experiment was run.

Their intentions in the present changed "random" clicks on a tape made in their past.

Remember *post hoc, ergo propter hoc*, "after it, therefore because of it"? We saw that this was false reasoning if we are not very careful about cause and effect. But here we have something more like "after it, therefore, the *cause* of it!"

McTaggart describes Schmidt's understanding of his weird results as follows:

> It wasn't that his participants had changed a tape after it had been created; their influence had reached "back in time" and influenced the [REG] machine's output at the moment that it was first recorded. They had changed the output of the machine in the same way they might have if they had been present at the time it was being recorded. They did not *change* the past from what it was; they *influenced the past when it was unfolding as the present* so that it *became* what it was.[15] [Emphasis in the original.]

We assume that if A caused B, then A occurred before B. But in Schmidt's experiments, and in many others McTaggart describes from the scientific literature, A caused B, but A occurred *after* B! This is clearly noodle-baking of the first rank, so what's going on?

The intent here is not to prove or disprove retrocausation; it's too early in the experimental game to draw any firm conclusions one way or another. What we have, though, is one possible explanation for how the backstage engineering of our local physical universe (or large chunks of it as we've seen) could have been done.

We have a powerful Agency that exists in an ontological reality outside our space-time universe. We were once consciously aware of it, and participated in the work we and it were doing here in Sunshine Corner. These times were called the Golden Age, and hundreds of stories and legends from around the world describe it. However, they also describe a physical

Sometimes, A can cause B, even if A comes after B!

cataclysm that ended it. An abundance of geological evidence places this event about 11,500 years ago. Being outside time as they are, the Agency would have had foreknowledge of it. A consultation is made between us and them. The cataclysm can't be prevented, all agree; grave damage is going to be done to physical Earth—in our ontological domain. We on this side are going to forget about our partners on the other side; both parties can "see" this, and thereafter we are going to be locked in a linear, experiential past-to-present-to-future time sense over here. The best that can be done "beforehand" is to leave clues in the very fabric of the physical universe that are easy for us to observe, sooner or later. In particular, engineering things so as to end up with the Moon having the same apparent size as the Sun to us observers here on Earth's surface, but along the way create all the other numerical patterns that we have seen (and possibly many more yet to be discovered). The Moon, for example, was created with the size, location and movements we observe today by affecting its creation *as it was unfolding as the present*, even if that took millions of years. Standing outside of the flow of time, long spans of local time aren't a problem: in for a dime, in for a dollar. But how would we/they do this?

By creating a powerful intention that it be so. The intention would stretch back as far into the past as would be necessary to make it be so. Such mundane tools as engineering drawings and computers wouldn't be necessary. Only awareness and focused intent. Archimedes said, "Give me a place to stand and a long enough lever, and I will move the Earth." Perhaps, our Agency, by standing outside our mundane, space-time reality, had a place to stand that gave them enough power to re-engineer our corner of the physical cosmos, as described, say, in our Backstage Theory. Being outside spacetime is their long lever. It might be very hard to substantially alter an oil painting if you are one of the objects depicted within it, but it is entirely another thing if you are the artist standing in front of it, paint and brushes in hand. This is the Agency's position *vis-à-vis* the physical world, and it was also perhaps our position before we lost the awareness of it, at least in our normal states of consciousness.

But, still. Retrocausation? No physicist in academia who values his or her career would endorse such a view. The reason is simple: formerly there was no evidence for it. On first exposure it just looks like making things up, like telling some kind of "just so" story to explain something to gullible people, something that physicists don't think even *needs* explaining. Yet, we have just gone through a long list of evidence that says something just like this has indeed happened. The problem is, this evidence is new and it's certainly incomplete. It *is* evidence, though, that something extraordinary happened to bring the conditions about that we have observed. At this point, all we can say one way or another is—insufficient data. Perhaps, though, retrocausation is merely quantum non-locality from a higher point of view.

The Forgetful Partner Theory

Automobiles are designed and created from two points of view. There is a designer who has the human body for his or her design target, while at the same time the human driver knows what is required from the designer in order to drive the car safely and comfortably. Usually, the designer is also a driver. The difference is, we know what cars are for, and we know somebody designed and built them. The "message" of the car is that we can get in it and drive it around. The mere presence of the car contains the message "you can drive me." Of course, we must have sufficient prior experience to know that that stubby, shiny thing is a vehicle for human transportation, how to get in it, how to start it up, and so on.

It is possible, though, that someone from a primitive or past society might not know what a car is, neither that it is a transportation vehicle (its purpose) nor even that it was designed and built to transport him somewhere (its message). It would be easy for this person to imagine the car was merely a small house—somewhere to get in out of the rain, store provisions and hide from enemies and predators.

Now to begin to bring this analogy full circle, imagine that this person lived in a modern city, but had suffered an accident, causing his loss of memory. In reality, he was one of the car's designers, but of this he remembers nothing, nor can he remember what cars are for. The message of the car—that it is to be driven—is lost on him. What's more, he has a very important job for which he *needs* a car. Sadly, he can't remember what his job is, either.

Forget the keys. Where'd I leave the car? (BTW, what's a car?)

The message of the car—that it's to be driven by him—indicates its purpose. The message of an artificial Solar System and human body—that some Agency somewhere and somewhen constructed it—also indicates its purpose:

- There is such an Agency, and
- our solar environment and most of our physical selves are artificial.
- Therefore, the "real" universe must include that Agency as a component, and
- effects and components of that Agency are in the world and in us.

Even if we (currently) can't contact or identify that Agency, the universe must include regions or levels that contain it. These regions are not separate from the physical universe we perceive; the different regions or levels must interpenetrate each other, of which fact the message is evidence. Our senses and instruments, therefore, cannot define a real limit to the universe, although they may appear to do so. The message itself has no such limits, therefore the universe has no such limits either. The message is embedded in and is a part of the physical world; it is also embedded in a non-observable world, which makes the universe qualitatively larger than it appears to us, because of the very existence of the message we have apprehended. And since we're baked in the same pie, within ourselves we must also include levels beyond the physical one that is sensible to us.

The real state of affairs differs from the billboard in the desert example in subtle but important ways. Consider instead the ending of Mel Brooks' wonderful movie *Blazing Saddles*. Most of the movie takes place in and around a small town in the old desert Southwest. The good guys and bad guys are cowboys, saloon girls and dirty government officials. (Has anything changed, one wonders?) Anyway, at the end of the movie, the town and all the characters are hilariously revealed to be on a movie set; in the last scene the two main actors dismount their horses and are driven away in a limousine. The movie company is the Agency that has constructed the town, the plot and all the roles for the actors. What is revealed is that the local desert environment was constructed, built and engineered to tell a false story. We see that what we think is the real world (well, fairly real) is in fact only part of a much larger world that exists in a perceptually different place and time—on a different ontological level: a modern-day Hollywood movie lot and nearby desert locations. All real, but fake. Not what they appear to be.

Watch Mel Brooks' Blazing Saddles again, immediately

In the situation we have been examining, the Solar System is the movie lot; the planets and Sun are props "constructed" by an Agency that corresponds to Mel's movie company. So, in a sense, are we. (One hopes, though, that Mel is not in charge of this other Agency!) The planets, Sun and so on are real, considered by themselves; we can live in the "movie" our whole lives, believing what our senses and instruments tell us about it. But once we see the message embedded in it, once we realize we are in kind of a movie ourselves, nothing can ever be the same. (Here's *The Matrix* again.) Even if we can't see backstage—the movie lot, the director and crew, etc.—we can see the evidence that there must be a backstage somewhere. Our goal now must be to find a way to contact someone in this Agency and find out what's really going on, what this movie—our lives—is really about.

This whole state of affairs we find ourselves in completely confounds both sides of the Anthropic debate. The physicists and astronomers can't explain the implications of their own numbers, so there is much foundational work to do in these disciplines; there is much to be added, as the universe is now seen to be qualitatively much different and much larger than they currently assume it is. Then the molecular biologists, geneticists and others must consider the human gestation period-water-lunar sidereal connection in other ways than being mere coincidences.

In many ways, though, the creationists are in worse shape. No longer is "God" just a sort of Fairy Godmother (er, Godfather?) with an extremely long magic wand, who somehow threw the universe together after a spark of inspiration. They must confront the fact that "God" was not only a mathematician, He/She/It was a crackerjack engineer who probably had lots of help. Who would be the most likely candidates for helpers? Why humans, of course. The best designer of a car is a human, and the best designer of an Earth/Moon-sized "car" is also a human.

"But," we reply, as the puny humans we seem to be, "such a thing is far beyond what we're capable of; it's almost beyond what we can conceive. Besides, that was God's job. We came along after all that was done."

Did we? It seems like we must have, but remember those *post hoc* assumptions and retrocausation. If we would be the best designers of our own cosmic environment, then the fact that we don't remember doing so— meaning we don't have any extant records or memories of doing so—is not to say we didn't help design it in fact. In the movies, if the dead guy is the only person who could have stolen the money, then he must not really be dead after all; the detectives must have overlooked or misunderstood some clues. In our earlier example, the driver of the car forgot he was also its designer; he forgot what the car was *for* and that is was *for* him.

Is the essence of the message that we have forgotten what our lives— collectively and individually—are for, and that there are some clues we have also overlooked and mistaken?

Creator vs. Created

What is real, and where does our "reality" come from? There are several possibilities that have been considered in different areas of inquiry.

1. RELIGION. If a monotheistic god created the universe, then from the technical view of most modern physicists, it isn't "natural." To them, natural means that there is no agency besides the physical forces and laws they have already observed, or such similar laws yet to be discovered. A creation by such a being, assuming one exists, would be artificial, not natural. Fake. To religious adherents, though, it doesn't matter how Creation is classified; it only matters that their Creator did his thing and we're the result. Here, however, the existence of such a Being is beyond our concern. All we wish to do is try to explain the existence and meaning of the numerical and related patterns we have gone over, and who and what caused/created them, which is a scope that is much smaller than questions of any ultimate origins of ourselves or our world. Our concerns are only with who twiddled what was already here and why they did it.

2. THEORETICAL PHYSICS. A novel view from certain theorists in modern physics is another possibility, which says there might be an infinite number of other universes—some like ours, some utterly different. This is called the Metaverse, in which these independent universes don't communicate with each other.[16] None of them can therefore be real the way we mean this because they all must be equally "real." In some of them, something just like the computer simulation in the film *The Matrix* might be going on: we humans live in a computer simulation and therefore aren't "real." There, we're nothing more than some deeply complex—and buggy—software. Definitely not real. But this is not what we're describing here. Instead, our Agency exists in a superset of our universe, in a part that is temporarily inaccessible to us due to an unavoidable cataclysm that happened millennia ago. What we may experience of it is just part of a much larger and grander reality, with which it *is* possible to re-establish communications.

3. SPIRITUALITY AND PHILOSOPHY. There is a position in Eastern traditions, at least as understood here in the West, that the universe is illusory; it has no real existence at all. This is the idea that everything we perceive with our senses to be "out there" is really "in here," inside our mind, which makes the whole outer world up. In Hinduism this concept is called *maya*, which means illusion—fakery, yet the real concept isn't as simple as this explanation. The problem with it is illustrated by the Zen master, as the story goes, who found it easiest to convey this

concept to his student by whacking him over the head with a two-by-four. By experience, then, the student discovered that skull, board and pain were all very real. The important question to be discovered is what exists beyond *maya*? Is there a part of reality that exists past the world of appearances? In many Eastern systems of thought, the answer is yes, and practices have been developed in those systems to allow practitioners to experience it. This exactly matches our approach here, where our numerical patterns replace the two-by-four to wake us up, and the Agency and its ontological realm represent what is beyond the *maya* of the physical universe. All that's missing here are some appropriate practices, which we'll get to shortly.

> *Zen Master whacks student with 2x4; says, "Real is real," then disappears into thin air.*

4. DIRECT OBSERVATION. The last alternative, the one we are advancing here, is that "reality" was contrived, altered, diddled, messed with—done in order to send us, stranded here in our physical reality, a message that this isn't all that exists, that more is within our reach. In essence, our "reality" is incomplete, just as the term *maya* means incomplete. We aren't really stranded; it just seems like it. There is a way to other realms of existence that are just as real, if not more real, than the world we experience. More complete means more real.

It can be difficult to choose from among these alternatives. The first two alternatives require belief in things that cannot be proven. God, in the first alternative, and mere mathematical speculation in the second. The existence of God is unprovable in the former, and the wild speculations of string theory, the big bang, inflation, dark matter and energy, and so on are untestable in the latter, making them unscientific. (Physics has long since jettisoned the requirement that a theory be backed up by experimental evidence. Theory has become fact without supporting evidence, exactly as God in heaven is said to exist without evidence. Popular science writers are some of the worst offenders, willing to offer the latest theories as Gospel, instead of the hypothetical ideas they really are.)

The last two alternatives have a lot in common. In fact, number 4, the thesis we're presenting here, is the same as number 3, with scientific observations in place of spiritual instruction and meditation, at least in these first steps. Admittedly, using math, astronomy and physics against the staunch materialists and humanists in those same scientific disciplines gives not a little sublime delight. (Not all physicists are so dogmatic. A few are searching in new directions, hoping that breakthrough paradigms will appear that will lead to solutions to a host of problems.) In the end, I think physics, as it stands today in myriad dead ends, will be subsumed into alternative 3, helped along, perhaps, by arguments like this one.

Symbols and Patterns

There is more to say about the circle and square we looked at in Chapter 1. I have repeated Figure 9 here for convenience. I omitted the radius line, but retained the implied center point of the original figure. This is more advanced material which had to wait until the idea of patterns was more fully developed. We're at that point now, so let's look more deeply at the implications of the major pattern number .2732, which we found was the ratio of the area of the gray corners to the area of the circle. What was the real motivation for arriving at this particular ratio? The answer involves the symbols of circle and square and their various meanings.

The Perfect Circle

The circle has always symbolized perfection. There are no sharp corners. Each point on the circumference is the same distance to the center point. A circle is the only geometric shape that implies steady, unimpeded movement. A circle rotates, and this rotational movement may even go unnoticed in some cases when the interior is unmarked. A circle also has an implied movement from center to circumference and back. The circle "breathes out" toward the perimeter, then "breathes in" toward the center, an unending cycle. We are reminded of respiration and the beating of the human heart.

In many myths and legends, the circle represents heaven, or unmanifest spiritual planes of being. It also represents spirit and eternity—the timeless realms with no beginning and no end.

More generally, circles and also spheres represent a center or central point. In particular, the circle often represents the Sun, which is the center of the Solar System. The circle has also been used to represent a state of Oneness and a state of inner harmony.

A circle, by virtue of its movement, represents that which brings many things into being and manifestation; it may be seen as that which activates and animates all the forces in any process.

Finally, a circle separates that which is inside from that which is outside. Inside is order and perfection; outside is chaos, disorder, and imperfection. Outside the circle lies danger, and real possibilities for strife, hazard, and disorganized energies.

The Manifest Square

A square is in many ways the direct opposite of a circle. It represents the physical, manifest world of four compass directions, four seasons, the four corners of the Earth, and the right angles of our buildings and artifacts. It is a figure of firmness, order, and stability; we say we stand "four square" behind some principle we deem important. We try to give someone a square shake or a square meal. The square and the cube—its three-dimensional brother—are the primary symbols of solidity and manifestation.

Above all, the square is the symbol for the Earth and mankind in general. In psychological terms, from an imperfect "square" state man strives, at least in some abstract way, to achieve a state of "circular" perfection. If you think about it, this implies that this perfect state already exists in in an unmanifest state, otherwise we wouldn't be able to conceive it. The circular perfection, then, always pre-exists the imperfect instantiation of it. Said another way, the lower derives from the higher, never the other way around.

Squaring the Circle

The circle often symbolically denotes the beginning of a process, and the square denotes its end. A cartoon man's idea is depicted as a circular light bulb above his head, and the completion or manifestation of that idea is something concrete and material he builds or does based on the idea. Without getting too philosophical, the ideas and potentialities our minds devise exist in a non-manifest, "circular" realm, if you will, while we give them physical existence at a later point in time. Composers such as Mozart and Beethoven could see and hear entire musical compositions in their heads before ever writing them down or playing them on an instrument. An artist can visualize the picture she is going to paint before ever laying brush to canvas. An architect may have a detailed view of the skyscraper he is designing, and good movie directors are able to visualize the look and visual details of each scene before the cameras roll.

Many, if not all, human endeavors begin with a plan and end with a final product, even if several iterations are needed before something satisfactory is achieved. This holds true for everything from a well-reasoned argument in a business meeting, to a football quarterback's instant-to-instant plan to throw, run or take a sack: his body carries out his mind's plan.

Let's look at the figure again. We started with the circle. Using what we now know about the symbolism of circles, here we have the starting point, the idea for the manifest world. Within the circle is the "location" from which the manifest world, symbolized by the square, was created. It is where the agents and creators reside; it is where all creations begin.

The figure gives us a way to visualize this. Imagine the four corner flaps of the square enfolded in the circle. We could start with just the circle and visualize the four corners resting at its center, completely unmanifest at this point. If we could then grab them and pull them outside the circle, the "squareness" of the full figure would become manifest.

The Number of Manifestation

What emerges—the four shaded corner areas—can be compared to what was formerly latent—the circle. We can measure this "emergence" by comparing the geometric area of the corners to the area of the circle. We did this by forming the ratio $(4 - \pi) / \pi$, which has the value .2732.

What is amazing are all the consistent echoes of this manifestation number, from the freezing temperature of water, to the measured energy of the cosmic microwave background radiation, to the human gestation period and all the rest. When we include the reciprocal number 3.66 and the related number 18.6, we see that the diagram of square and inscribed circle give a quantifiable, numerical value to the process of physical manifestation. Moreover, it also shows the handiwork of some agency that inserted order into the normal chaos and randomness of the world for our benefit and, above all, to produce us humans in the first place.

Were we complicit in all this, but have just forgotten about it? The characters depicted on a canvas can't assist in their own creation unless they help guide the hand of the artist by somehow coming out of the picture. This could only happen if the phrase, "Be all you can be" really means, "Be a lot more than you ever imagined."

More noodle baking, for sure, unless we loosen our mental pictures of who we are and how we came to be, and enlarge them to include the implications of all we've discussed up to now. It is easy—and tempting—to discard some or all of the data and simply declare, "No, no, this just can't be right." But it is dishonest to do so.

Fine. It's time to make a beeline for a new paradigm that rhymes. (Sorry. Couldn't resist.)

And in the Beginning ...

What we lack in our knowledge of how this all might have come about is the starting place. We don't know, for example, if the nature of space and time was ironed out first, which was the assumption in the Backstage Theory, or if our own natures as human beings came first and then the local universe was designed around us, "for" us and with our help. This second type of process (without the human aid part, of course) was held by the Catholic Church for centuries, until the time of Galileo. The Earth was held to be the center of the universe, and all was created for our sakes. It turned out not to be true, so everyone assumed that humankind, which lives on the Earth, couldn't be its center either. After all, look at us! Who'd want to waste an entire Creation on people who despise each other, can't find the lowest price on car insurance and watch too much reality TV? Nonetheless, we weren't always like this. There was once a Golden Age when we all lived in harmony and had important jobs to do for the planet—until something went horribly wrong. To see the consequences of this, let's get back to something we left hanging a bit earlier: the Mini-Anthropic Principle.

Creator scratches head; wonders if it was worth it.

What if we *are* the center of this corner of the universe—our planet Earth? What if we have a purpose here of which we are no longer aware? Suppose we were engaged in this purpose during that Golden Age, since we were then full participants in that Agency's business, but then some calamity happened in Earth's past that ended that Golden Age. This would have to have happened in fairly recent human times, not geological time, so that the memory of both the Golden Age and the cataclysm would remain, as it has in creation myths and legends from around the world; it would have to have happened after humans were living on Earth. There is a great deal of scientific evidence to support such a view.[17] In summary, an object or force of

The Golden Age and the Cataclysm

some kind (a massive solar or extra-solar electrical disturbance, perhaps) struck the Earth about 11,500 years ago. There is widespread evidence for something like this across the entire Northern Hemisphere, evidence of massive floods and winds that swept living animals thousands of miles, gigantic lightning storms, and the bombardment of hundreds of objects that struck Earth from space. As a result, much animal and human life on Earth was lost.

Suppose that prior to this cataclysm our consciousness encompassed and included those beings we have been referring to as an Agency. In other words, at that time, being human meant existing both here on the physical Earth and existing in another ontological domain where such things as Solar System engineering are possible. When the cataclysm struck Earth, our human consciousness was almost completely severed from our Agency consciousness, and we, stranded here on Earth, eventually forgot our own former abilities, as no one—or very few—still retained them. We forgot about the existence of our other halves.

From the Agency's point of view, we were stranded, tossed overboard, away from one half of an existence we could no longer perceive. What to do? Throw us a "life" preserver that would help us remember. So we/they—their half of the severed entity—proceeded to engineer a message into the very structure of our astronomical environment for our half. If the Agency—our other halves—stands outside the confines of space and time, which is perhaps why we can't locate them, it would be possible to do the necessary backstage engineering while *at the same time* knowing what the results of such work would have to be. This corresponds to a painter modifying her painting in real time, thereby changing her subject's whole environment. Linear cause and effect would no longer apply; they/we would be cause and effect at the same "time," since they operated outside time as we experience it. This scenario would be

> *We have met the Agency, and it is us. (Apologies to Walt Kelly and Pogo)*

analogous to a movie company arriving in town and altering, creating and moving certain things to suit the purpose of the movie they were preparing to shoot. The people already in the town might easily be unaware of these preparations, just as we would be unaware of an Agency's preparations in and around the Solar System, especially if they occurred just after a major cataclysm when we, as its victims, were distracted (to say the least), which provided the motive for such message-bearing alterations in the first place. For this reason, getting such a message through to us, stuck here on the physical side of an existence divide, must have been exceedingly important.

And it would be most important to those who were impacted the most—ourselves. Unable to help ourselves for a long time afterward—up to now, in fact—we would have to have assistance from the other side, this Agency.

Where is this assistance, you say? Well, now we have to get away from the numbers a bit. First of all, very small children are aware of a lot that they forget as adults. What are all those newborns staring at besides mama and daddy? The same things some dying people see; people at both edges of life. But by age six all awareness of non-ordinary reality is scrubbed out of us, a process psychologists call enculturation. I like Don Miguel Ruiz's term better: in his bestseller *The Four Agreements* he calls it domestication. However, this extra awareness doesn't ever entirely leave us, and some people manage to retain or regain it as adults—something that will interest us as we go on a little further. There are lots of cracks in the world where Agency-originated messages come through; we call some of these hunches, the sixth sense, intuition, the small, quiet voice inside of us, our conscience, and so on. The messages are there, all right; the question is do we hear them and listen to them?

Being domesticated primates ain't a guaranteed good thing, you guys.

Or more to the point, can we learn to?

Back to the numbers and patterns we've found in our Solar environment. If someone went to all the trouble to construct such a message, wouldn't they also embed in that message the means to repair the damage to our consciousness, under the post-cataclysmic conditions that then prevailed and still do? Wouldn't they provide some hint of how to bridge the divide that separates our two halves? Of course they would. Strewn among the numerical hints in the message, it didn't take long to find it.

The hint has to involve the part of the message that most pertains to us—to our physical bodies—and it will certainly contain our new natural constant, 0.2732 somewhere. Our bodies are 70% water. Going back, therefore, to the Centigrade temperature scale which was based on water, the salient number is that of absolute zero, -273.2°C. When we recall that this is the temperature at which all random thermal molecular motion ceases, it is not hard to see how this hint applies to our own conscious states. We are always running off at the mind—there is the seemingly ceaseless chatter going on in our heads, of first one thing then another. If physical absolute zero means no molecular motion, then mental absolute zero must mean no mental "motion." A still mind. Which implies a mind at peace. An inner state of clarity and quiet, wherein our long-lost other half may still be apprehended, for whatever the cataclysm was, it didn't cut off all communication with this Agency—otherwise we would no longer be human beings at all, but only non-self-aware primates. It merely lowered the conscious volume of the connection between halves. Achieving a still mind is not the only step necessary for re-establishing contact with our other selves, but it is the first step.

Nevertheless, could it really be this simple? Could the message not only tell us that there is more to reality than our senses and instruments reveal—and do it with hard, scientific numbers and not airy-fairy wishful thinking (and my apologies to the faeries)—but also tell us exactly how to transcend that limited view of reality and enter into a much more expansive one? At least tell us how to take the first step?

The message in a Solar System

It is not my intent to waste your time and mine with yet another theory that can't be proven; one that isn't testable and falsifiable. All the numerical data presented here can be found in standard references (or Wikipedia, for example), and an ordinary calculator will run the numbers. But determining or refuting the proof of the content and presence of the message requires a different approach. You must put down your references, your calculator and your instruments, close your eyes and begin the work of quieting your mind, for the proof lies not at the far end of a telescope, but behind the eyepiece of the near end, in your own mind.

5

CONTACTING THE AGENCY

*I*S THE EFFORT to establish contact with the Agency for yourself worth it? And what was that earlier about having important jobs to do for the planet that we have forgotten about? What kind of jobs? Everybody? To properly understand such jobs requires making conscious contact with this Agency. After all, most jobs can't even be started unless we show up. If we showed up on the other side of the divide, how much more of these important jobs might we understand? And as you have surmised by now, showing up doesn't mean blasting off in a rocket to somewhere, but rather quietly and steadily blasting into your mind, to the location where that bridge between ontological realms once stood, and rebuilding it little by little.

There are definite steps you can take to contact the Agency—to recover awareness of the lost parts of yourself, if you'd like.

Encountering the "Agency"

Let's not be coy at this point. Down through the ages this so-called "Agency" has been known—to our modern sensibilities, let us note—with religious or at least spiritual overtones, and if we were to stick with these connotations by using religious words or concepts, many people would say, "Forget it. I'm not interested in that." Also, these terms would be misleading as we understand them today. Solar System Construction, Inc. *No harp music allowed* is a matter-of-fact, scientific and technological operation with offices in all fifty states, as it were. Actually, it's a multi-global organization, as we've been hinting at all along. So to talk about its agents as some kind of distant, non-engaged, aloof beings who are only interested in dead people—would be a big mistake. They are not milquetoast cloud-jockeys playing slow, boring harp music. They are engineers and artificers—creators—of immense benevolence. But above all, they are beings who desire personal relationships with each one of us, and so necessarily come in as many shapes and sizes as we do.

But perhaps an example.

One hot day in the summer of 1995 I was visiting a friend's house in Camp Verde, Arizona. She and her father had lived near the banks of the Verde River for many years, a small, shallow river, broad and slow, that flowed even during the hottest months.

It was my second day in Arizona, having come down from Colorado for a meeting. During that day she and I had done some testing on the effects of some musical tunings I was experimenting with. After work, we were joined by a few others, and we were just lazing in the back yard, no one being too anxious to start working on dinner, as the heat of the day had just broken. A cooling breeze floated in off the river, which meandered just out of sight past the cottonwoods beyond her backyard to the south.

I stepped away from the others to think about the music I had been playing that day. It was dusk—a gloaming that was already a bit indistinct. As I looked out toward the river I became aware that a group of tall people were looking at me from the middle distance. They were hard to see in the semi-darkness, yet I did see them. None of us moved. They were *very* tall—maybe twelve or fourteen feet. They were impossibly tall, thin and … translucent. They weren't people at all, at least not people like us. All I could do was stare at them. They stirred a little, but mostly just stared back at me.

In Which a Shocking Switcheroo Occurs

Even now, many years later, I'm not sure how many of them there were—my guess was seven or eight, although there could have been eleven or twelve. They were indistinct beings from a certain perspective, although mighty and definite from another. They stood side by side gazing at me, not sixty feet away. I became still, not wanting to frighten either them or myself with movement. I did look over at my friends on the patio, but they were engaged in talk, and weren't paying any attention to me.

These—*others* —though, were giving me their full attention. Since then I have often wondered why, and have concluded it had to do with the music that would ultimately result from my work at that time. Much later I discovered there were other reasons, having to do with duty and my own *job*, but it is not proper to speak of this here. It's enough to say that these beings intended to challenge me with their presence, for I knew they were *letting* me see them; they were definite, open, immediate, and were defiantly allowing themselves to be noticed.

But can they play b-ball?

Finally, I decided to call over to my friends on the patio, and I asked if anyone else saw what I was seeing. I pointed to where these *others* stood, but no one else saw them. After this, they gradually faded from my sight, and I have not seen them in a waking state again.

What actually happened? I certainly have no proof that several very tall beings made themselves visible to me for a few moments. They were only "real" to me; my friends that were there at the time couldn't see them. What is real, though, and lasting, is the gratitude I feel having been allowed to see them, and sense of commitment this experience left with me.

Who were they? Although I don't know directly, years later I found this description by W. Y. Evans-Wentz in his 1911 book *The Fairy Faith in Celtic Countries*. What follows are excerpts from his interview with an Irish mystic and seer.

A.– 'The beings whom I call the *Sidhe* [pronounced *Shee*], I divide, as I have seen them, into two great classes: those which are shining, and those which are opalescent and seem lit up by a light within themselves. The shining beings appear to be lower in the hierarchies; the opalescent beings are more rarely seen, and appear to hold the positions of great chiefs or princes among the tribes of Dana.' [...]

Q.– Can you describe one of the opalescent beings?

A.– 'The first of these I saw I remember very clearly, and the manner of its appearance: there was at first a dazzle of light, and then I saw that this came from the heart of a tall figure with a body apparently shaped out of half-transparent or opalescent air, and throughout the body ran a radiant, electrical fire, to which the heart seemed the center. Around the head of this being and through its waving luminous hair, which was blown all about the body like living strands of gold, there appeared flaming wing-like auras.' [...]

Q.– You speak of the opalescent beings as great beings; what stature do you assign to them, and to the shining beings?

A.– 'The opalescent beings seem to be about fourteen feet in stature, though I do not know why I attribute to them such definite height, since I had nothing to compare them with; but I have always considered them as much taller than our race. The shining beings seem to be about our own stature or just a little taller. Peasant and other Irish seers do not usually speak of the *Sidhe* as being little, but as being tall …[18]

Although I was only vaguely aware of the light around the beings I saw, this description of opalescent beings fits the beings I saw very closely: They were faeries—one variety of beings I've been calling the Agency. The quaint Victorian image of tiny beings, flitting among flowers comes from the Christian attempt to suppress and belittle the personal experiences of thousands of ordinary people in Ireland, Scotland and elsewhere. If some of these beings have appeared as small, it's because they chose to appear that way; their natural height is as described above. My ancestors come from the Highlands of Scotland, so perhaps this is why they chose to appear to me as they did. Your mileage may vary should you have a similar experience.

The Highlands of harmony

I knew their appearance somehow had to do with the music. The harmonies of the music I had been exploring all day had brought these beings here. Much later, I thought maybe they had always been (and always are) around; it was the music that had *retuned* me so that I was able to see them. No words were spoken, but as I looked at them a chill ran down my spine: they had come for the music, just as I had, and they had stayed long enough to thank me—with the definite implication that I was going to have to finish what I had started that day—one of my first "jobs." Two years later I did finish the project and produced a CD.[19] (All I have to say about them is Boy! were they ever patient with me, because completing that project and many others since then have been anything but easy or straightforward.)

So here's the switcheroo: We've left the impersonal, objective realm of numbers and the orbs of the Solar System and have necessarily bumped squarely into a very subjective, personal realm in our attempt to discover something definite about the Agency we've identified. You will just have to deal with this rude and sudden expansion of your sensibilities—and good luck to you in your endeavor. Because if you've come this far it's no more mere arms-length science for you, no siree, Bob. It's no more its-all-out-there theories, no more dualism. For me it turned into an intimate, inner quest for this Agency long ago, and it will for you too, if it hasn't already.

84

For look carefully. Did you have one of those so-called "imaginary" playmates when you were a child? I did. This experience near the Verde River wasn't exactly my first. These "agents"—by whatever names you chose to call them—are with us all the time. We can willfully opt to ignore them, and push them out of our conscious awareness, but we can also bring them back.

If we care to.

Perhaps you remember Jim Carry's character in *The Truman Show* movie. He lived all of his life in an artificial dome, where five thousand cameras televised every corner of his life around the clock—all choreographed and directed by a deliciously *Truman* evil Ed Harris. But Truman eventually finds out all his *escapes* life so far has been fake, and following some harrowing *his dome* trials at the end where the director tries to sink his sailboat in an artificial storm, he finds the edge of the dome—his entire world up to that moment—and exits through a conveniently-placed door.

Here's how to break out of your own dome. There are two steps.

The first is *Peace*: maintain a calm, inner, peaceful state, regardless of what's going on around you. It means learning to be a witness.

The second is to *Be still*: quiet the mind's inner chatter; still the inner voice that constantly speaks, sings, replays, and so on, inside your head.

It's a lot easier than rocket science.

Peace

We're not talking about world peace or anything else "out there." *Peace* here means essentially that we don't get sucked into the emotions and thoughts around us, nor those from our past, or speculations about the future. It means being an objective witness, not a participant who gets emotionally hooked. It means learning to be present—right here, right now. This is another way of saying Be Here Now, but this is why. If we get hit with emotions triggered by someone near us, and we get hooked into them, we can't be present; we are carried away by emotions or thoughts as we mentally relive some past event, or project what we think is a probable future event.

The practice of creating inner peace just means this: We can observe our thoughts and emotions, but without passion. We must be an observer of our thoughts; we must be a witness to whatever comes into our minds, and not get hooked by it. We can remember, but not replay. To do this, we create an observing center in ourselves. With a little practice, we can learn to sense thoughts and emotions coming and merely look at them as if from a distance. For—when we observe ourselves closely, we always have a split second to decide to get hooked by something, or let it pass. Take anger as an example. We can experience anger from another person and just think, "Oh, that's interesting. This time I don't have to get angry back." Or, we might be apprehensive about a business meeting tomorrow, but merely think, "Oh, it's interesting that I'm worried about this," and not get hooked into the worry right now. Of course the worry won't help; it might even cramp our style or limit our ability to catch a creative solution. But this sort of thing isn't what I'm getting at. It is stopping all internal thoughts for the sake of stopping them.

I remember an "anger" experience from many years ago, where I didn't think about what I was doing in the here-and-now; I wasn't watching myself and I got hooked, but good. My wife Pam and I *Don't ever do this!* were at a two-day seminar at Asilomar, a conference center in Monterey, California. I forget who the speaker was now, but he asked us to split into pairs for an exercise. So we paired up as did about forty other people. In our pairs we were each to take turns. First one would stand and turn to the other one, shake a finger, and say as angrily as we could, "Don't ever do that again!"

Now I don't remember why he asked us to do this, but it doesn't matter. I did it without thinking. I wasn't observing myself dispassionately and neutrally. Instead I got hooked by an authority figure, and did exactly what he told me to. Of course, there was no "that" act that anyone had done; the point was we all said it without thinking. (I think I said it. Pam said I caught myself in time, but I don't remember. I *do* remember the angry emotion of it, concentrated by all of us together. Ugh. It was terrible.)

To achieve inner peace you are to become a witness to yourself and the world. You are to say, "Oh, this is interesting. I was going to allow myself to get angry now, but this time I won't. Cool." In the Bible, the figure of Jesus counsels that you should "turn the other cheek." We commonly think this means he was meek, or mild. A sissy or a coward. It doesn't mean that at all. It means we are to turn away from anger. Not stick out the other cheek and dare the guy to hit us again, but to turn away inside ourselves and not participate in his anger, or whatever the emotion or train of thinking is at the moment. Turn away.

Of course, you must not judge. No judgment means being emotionally and mentally neutral—neutral toward both yourself and others. Another word for this is love—the highest kind there is.

This is hard. First, because it's often hard to remember to do this. It also requires you to be very brave, because often you must go against social or cultural norms. "No. Just because everybody else does it, doesn't mean I will." So second, it's hard to not do what your peers are doing. The payoff, though, is that by becoming a neutral observer you have taken the first step toward allowing the Agency to contact you. Being dispassionate is hard at first, but it gets easier with practice. You have tons of help in this, even if you can't see it yet.

The effects of becoming an observer will spread through your life amazingly rapidly. You will not be able to take my word for this; you will have to experience it for yourself. There are definite benefits, though, from not getting hooked into the world or into yourself. Sometimes this means making a choice: either jump into another's "stuff" or stay disengaged, even impersonal.

You can't do any lasting good in the world if you are not able to avoid getting hooked into negative emotions and situations. The airlines, for example, know this. They say that if there is a drop in cabin pressure, the oxygen masks will drop down, but the parent must put her mask on first, then her child's mask. Why? Because if she passes out, she won't be able to get either mask on and they both might pass out or worse. We can't help either ourselves or others from the middle of a situation that grabs us like Br'er Rabbit's Tar Baby. You can't pull someone out of quicksand if you are also in it. You need to be on solid ground before pulling on the rope will do any good.

A little aphorism sums this up:

Witnessing is the soul of compassion.

You can't be compassionate if you are wallowing in sentiment or emotion. You can't *act*. You can only be sucked in, which is not helpful. Indeed, if you want to help or be helped by the Agency, you're never going to be able to hear it or access it from within anger, or any other all-consuming thought or emotion. Compassion requires you to be in a neutral state.

But what about when another person wrongs you with some deed, or even cutting or hurtful words? This is even harder. How can you be detached now? How can you not lash back in kind, or at least not take the negative barb inside yourself, "to heart"? By forgiving them. Which can be stated in a second aphorism:

Forgiveness is the heart of compassion.

Of course, it is not only forgiving others. Perhaps more often, you must forgive yourself. This is the last piece of the imperative, "Peace." Being a true witness of the world and yourself involves forgiveness at every step. What might help here is to pick up a copy of Don Miguel Ruiz's *The Four Agreements* that I mentioned earlier if you don't already have it on your shelf. His second and third agreements are all about this. In fact, these are the first step in every genuine spiritual tradition.

To forgive yourself means letting all the negativity come up that is buried deep within once and for all and neutralizing it from your new stance of objective witnessing. "Sure, I did that thing, or that thing happened to me, but that was then and this is now, and now everything's different. I am different, too." It's nothing that needs to bring you down any more.

The cost of no longer getting hooked is high. The cost can be most of who you are. But the payoff! You will find, if nothing else, that from mastering this step the universe will gradually begin to operate on your behalf. To repeat that a little louder:

The universe will gradually begin to operate on your behalf.

This means that things will begin to get better. It is impossible, probably, for you to believe this without trying it. But try not getting hooked on anything external or internal for a few weeks and see for yourself what happens. Until then, you'll just have to trust me. Fair warning, though: If you are really in neutral, your ego is neutralized. This mean that what you previously wanted for yourself is also neutralized. New wants/needs appear that are not wholly your own anymore. You are now available for service to something beyond yourself, and for this the Agency will help you achieve your/their now-common goals. This is why, incidentally, all that New Age hoo-haw about *The Secret* never worked. You must first kill the ego by stages so that what *does* work can come to the surface.

So that's what "Peace" means. Try to remember yourself; see yourself from an inner observation post. Practice being in neutral. Say to yourself, "Oh, that's interesting," and let whatever it is go. Remember, but don't replay. Aim for a steady, inner peaceful state. Try to hold it—and remember to hold it—as long as you can.

Only when you can do this can you go on to the next imperative: Be still.

Be Still

To be still doesn't mean to avoid fidgeting in your chair or not bumping the person next to you. It means allowing your thoughts to come to a halt. It means getting your mind out of the way so the Agency has a chance to contact you. "But, Fred," perhaps you say, "won't I just make stuff up that I selfishly really want to do? How would this be any different?"

It is different, because if you have become adept at being at peace within yourself you'll find that your old thoughts, feelings and wishes have become different. This is one of the effects of *the detachment of peace*, and it's why Being Still is step two, not step one. You have to get your ego and your neuroses out of the way, first. Then next, you must work at dispatching the thoughts that come up. Here's how.

To learn how to do this, you'll need to sit quietly where you won't be disturbed. Later you can do this anywhere, but do it this way for now. Sit up straight and don't fall asleep. Close your eyes, take some deep breaths and observe your thoughts. As soon as the first one comes up, say something like, "Okay, I see that," and let it go. Don't spend any time with it. Let it dissolve behind you. Let it be swept away. You can devise your own symbolic way of doing this, but make it swift. Don't linger; the goal is to let each thought go as it arises. While you're doing this don't replay any experiences—emotional or otherwise—that the thought recalls. Just observe it then toss it away.

Pretty soon new thoughts won't come as fast. There will be moments of emptiness where you don't have any thoughts. This is good. Concentrate on your breath to keep you present. Once you experience this space, you will begin to want it more often. It's a very cool thing you can do for yourself.

Note this, however. When your Agency guides detect that you're listening, they start handing out jobs. These jobs have responsibilities, but they also have perks that no other kinds of jobs have. Did I mention that

The universe will gradually begin to operate on your behalf.

If you have checked your ego at the door, there is no telling how this may manifest for you. *I* certainly don't know. But *you* will know, that's for sure. I can only offer this one little caveat. Once you begin to get an idea of which jobs the Agency has in mind for you, it's too late to turn back. Of course, you can choose not to do them for a while. You can hold out. Resist. Maybe you'll be scared. Maybe you'll think you couldn't possibly do what they're suggesting you do. Deep inside, though, you know you can. The Agency knows what you can handle, even if you must stretch yourself. Remember that all the Agency's jobs benefit (and do not harm) other people in addition to benefitting you. This latter is a job perk—you benefit, too.

How will you know for sure? Well, you'll have to be paying attention to what's going on around you. This will happen naturally as a direct result of your constant attention to not getting hooked by events. You have to watch events, but suppose, say, a book nearly falls off the shelf when you walk by? Suppose a stranger says something to you, or you have an irresistible urge to speak to one? Suppose something flickers in the corner of your eye and you turn to see what it is? Suppose you have a powerful, new dream?

If it involves harming no one, it is likely, "Agency calling."

Sphere Music

We left a bit of evidence unexamined back in Chapter 2 that we now need to come back to. Recall that 109.3 Earths fit side-by-side across the Sun's diameter, and that 109.3 Suns fit in Earth's orbital radius. This new number 109.3 equals 4 x 27.32, our old pattern number, a fact which we left hanging. It's time to take a look at this number more closely.

The first thing that is bothersome is that factor of four. Throwing an arbitrary number in without any apparent reason is too much like making something up—a fudge factor—so that some random fact only then fits the argument, something which is not acceptable here. What we need, therefore, is ask if there's a way to naturally account for this odd 4? There is, and it has to do with sound and music.

Consider now that 27.32 represents a sound frequency. Frequencies are measured in cycles or vibrations per second, commonly called Hertz, named after the nineteenth-century physicist Heinrich Hertz. A frequency of 27.32 Hertz or just Hz describes a certain very low pitch, close to the lowest limit of human hearing. (The upper limit is about 20,000 Hz.)

Doubling a frequency moves the pitch up one octave; this is like moving from the lowest A note on a piano to the next higher A. Two frequencies (pitches) one octave apart sound similar—harmonic—to our ears. Doubling the frequency again (so times 4 altogether) brings us to another A—at 109.3 Hz, in the range of a bass-baritone voice. So we have the same "sounding" notes at different integer multiples of 27.32 Hz—thus naturally accounting for the factor of four. 109.3 Hz is the same note as 27.32 Hz, just up two octaves. Up two more octaves we reach 437.2 Hz, which used to be the concert pitch (called A) used by symphony orchestras. (It has since moved up a bit to an A of 440 Hz.) We can go on up octaves in this manner until we exceed the limits of human hearing.

What we would now like to ask is, if among all these octaves, there is something special about the number we started with in relation to the Earth and Sun, which was 109.3? There is, for the Agency has left us another clue. The first clue was that we are to quiet the inner movement in our minds—our mind chatter—just as lowering the temperature to absolute zero (-273.2°C) stills all molecular movement in a substance. Here, though, we are to look at what happens to our minds when a pitch near 109 Hz is played. To begin to understand this, we have to go back six thousand years to the island of Malta in the Mediterranean Sea.

Here are found perhaps the world's oldest megalithic temples; they are at least a millennium older than Stonehenge or the Pyramids. Of the more than thirty known sites, five remain amazingly intact. One of these is a subterranean site hewed out of soft limestone. The architectural features of these temples are unprecedented: courtyards, retaining walls, corbelling, curved inner walls, and horizontal arches. But their most amazing features are acoustic ones. The underground temple remains essentially intact, including its ceiling. It is called the Hal-Saflieni Hypogeum, meaning a "haunting place of dreams and secrets."

Overseen now by UNESCO, access is limited to ten people per hour. According to archeologist Linda Eneix,

> Standing in the Hypogeum is like being inside a giant bell. At certain pitches, one feels the sound vibrating in bone and tissue as much as hearing it in the ear. It's actually quite thrilling. As anyone who sings in the shower knows, sound echoing back and amplifying itself from hard surfaces can do unusual things. That effect is hugely magnified in Malta's limestone chambers.[20]

Archaeo-acoustics is the merging of archaeology and sound science. Many megalithic sites have been investigated for their acoustic behavior. A consortium from Princeton University found that the sites they studied all sustained a strong resonance at a sound frequency between 95 and 120 Hz. In many underground sites, including the Hypogeum on Malta, the strongest resonant frequency is 110 Hz—just a hair away from our pattern number 109.3, so close as to be sensibly the same frequency. The salient point here is what happens to our brain/mind in these chambers, or when exposed to this frequency. According to findings from a UCLA researcher in 2008,

> brain activity in a number of healthy volunteers was monitored by EEG through exposure to different resonant frequencies. Their findings indicated that at 110 Hz the patterns of activity over the prefrontal cortex abruptly shifted, resulting in a relative deactivation of the language center and a temporary shifting from left to right-sided dominance related to emotional processing.[21]

A "resonant" frequency is one that reinforces itself in the chamber or object in which it occurs. A tuning fork is a simple example: it vibrates at a frequency determined by the dimensions of its construction. In a chamber like the Hypogeum (and also Stonehenge and other megalithic sites, researchers believe), standing waves occur at the resonant frequencies, determined by, for example, the distance between opposite walls or large stones that face each other. Next, what does "deactivation of the language center" mean? It is this language center that constantly talks to us, sings to us, and "thinks" to us. To turn it off is to turn off our left-brain, inner mental chatter—exactly the goal when seeking to achieve inner stillness.

It isn't necessary to visit a megalithic site to experience this effect. The acoustic properties of many of these sites suggest that, among other things, they were used to induce altered states of consciousness during rituals when certain specific sounds were played. The same sorts of altered states can be created with modern technology. A digital synthesizer and many different audio computer programs can easily create sounds and music that do this—although the effectiveness of such music in stilling the mind is highly variable. This book's companion web site[22] has some sounds and music you can try for yourself.

Schumann Resonance for Hummies

Our program here is to establish that there is a universal or cosmic level of consciousness that we are no longer able to easily access. I have represented this as an Agency which is intimately interested in reestablishing the connection between us and them. Once there was such a connection, 12,000 or more years ago, which allowed a Golden Age to exist. It then ceased, or was severely attenuated, by a cataclysm which had definite, catastrophic physical elements, but also had very much less well-understood subtle consequences that affected the scope of our consciousness. What we'd like to consider now is this: Is there any corroboration of this broken connection, using our pattern numbers? There is, and it concerns the frequency 27.3 Hz.

We need to look at the Earth as a whole for this part of the investigation, specifically Earth's atmosphere. We humans move in a largely-unseen "sea" of air. Ordinary air is a mixture of gasses such as nitrogen, oxygen, and so on, plus dust motes and other particulate matter—but it is much more than this. The atmospheric region forms an active electromagnetic envelope around us. Vibrating electromagnetic fields exist between Earth's surface and one of the upper layers of the atmosphere called the ionosphere (from about 30 to over 600 miles up—it is where auroras appear). The ground and the ionosphere form a cavity in which electromagnetic waves, generated primarily by lightning discharges, resonate with certain definite low frequencies. These are called Schumann resonant frequencies, the most powerful of which is 7.83 Hz. But there are several other frequency peaks that run up to about 50 Hz. These peaks are separated by about 6.5 Hz, and the series runs 7.8, 14.3, 20.8, then—surprise!—27.3 Hz.

I believe I heard my own jaw drop when I first encountered this fact. Octave harmonics are always present in any kind of waveform more complex than a simple sine wave, and there are plenty of harmonics present in our atmospheric waveguide, so the two-octave harmonic of 27.3—which, remember, is 109 Hz—naturally occurs in our atmosphere. It's around us all the time. But then, why aren't our minds put in a state of natural stillness if this frequency is present? Because it is overshadowed by a host of other frequencies that have just the opposite effect: they churn up our mental chatter and so keep us disconnected. Among the different Schumann frequencies, 27.3 Hz is well down the power curve from the much stronger 7.8 Hz frequency, where the octave harmonics occur at 62.4 Hz then 124.8 Hz—nothing even close to 109 Hz.

93

Neuroscientists have established that low frequency audio sounds entrain our internal brain rhythms. This is called the frequency-following response (FFR). So if 109 Hz was heard more strongly, our minds might naturally be a great deal more still without any effort, and we therefore might be able to communicate with the Agency a great deal more easily. But other, stronger signals entrain our brains away from this frequency, hence the constant inner self-talking.[23]

There is a tantalizing question here. If the number 27.3, expressed as a frequency, and its octave sibling 109 Hz, are present as naturally-occurring atmospheric frequencies, why *aren't* they stronger? Why are they drowned out by other, unhelpful, even (in this context) harmful, frequencies? The answer might have to do with some hitherto unknown side-effects of the global cataclysm we've discussed. The ionosphere exists primarily due to ultraviolet radiation coming from the Sun. Part of the ionosphere is a plasma, meaning it consists of atoms which have temporarily lost one or more electrons, so plasmas carry diffuse, but possibly very strong, electric fields. The ionosphere is in constant motion due to atmospheric wind currents and thermal radiation coming from the Sun—diurnal heating and cooling. A moving electric field always produces magnetic fields, and it is well-established that we humans are very sensitive to ambient magnetic fields.[24] Our mode of consciousness, even our motor functions, are dependent, then, on the electromagnetic activity between here and the Sun.

What if, during the Golden Age, the Sun emitted radiation that created dominant 27.3 and 109 Hz frequencies in Earth's atmosphere so that our inner mind chatter was much less, and our inner "ears" were much more attuned to the Agency, permitting brisk and clear two-way communication between we humans, tuned into the material realm, and the Agents, tuned into a different level of reality? Both parties would thereby experience a unitary "us." A conscious bridge, ladder or stairway would connect these levels that could perhaps be traversed at will. Then, what if this cataclysm— which we suspect was composed at least in part of a very large plasma— permanently altered the Sun's radiation, or altered the nature of our atmosphere, or altered some other aspect of the greater solar environment, effectively destroying this bridge and ending the Golden Age contact with the Agency?

Here's an odd thing. There is something called the Hum. That's right, with a capital letter. According to Wikipedia,

The Hum is a phenomenon, or collection of phenomena, involving a persistent and invasive low-frequency humming, rumbling, or droning noise not audible to all people. Hums have been widely reported by national media in the UK and the United States. The Hum is sometimes prefixed with the name of a locality where the problem has been particularly publicized: e.g., the "Bristol Hum", the "Taos Hum", or the "Bondi Hum" …

The essential element that defines the Hum is what is perceived as a persistent low-frequency sound, often described as being comparable to that of a distant diesel engine idling, or to some similar low-pitched sound for which obvious sources (e.g., household appliances, traffic noise, etc.) have been ruled out.[25]

This Hum doesn't seem to be connected with tinnitus or ringing in the ears. It's strength is apparently dependent on location; it's more pronounced and noticed by more people at certain places, such as Taos, New Mexico.[26] Interestingly, though, this hum seems to disappear inside subterranean limestone caves , such as, perhaps, the Hypogeum on Malta. Did those ancients build their sound chamber underground 6,000 years ago to escape bombardment of undesirable atmospheric frequencies? And where they then generated tones around 109 Hz during ceremonies by low chanting, singing, or with specially-tuned musical instruments? There is apparently some specific audio research to be done, I'd say.[27]

There's another method you can easily try—with or without these sounds or music—to achieve inner stillness. It just involves breathing.

Breath Work

There is a practice from Kundalini Yoga I'd like to give you. It has many benefits, one of which is to help you cut off your mind-chatter. It is an alternate breathing practice of pranayama.

The primary purpose of pranayama is to induce mental tranquility as a means to meditation. Tantra has this to say about pranayama:

The word pranayama means to extend and overcome one's normal limitations. It provides the method whereby one is able to attain higher states of vibratory energy. In other words, one is able to activate and to regulate the prana [subtle energy] comprising the human framework and thereby make oneself more sensitive to vibrations in the cosmos and within.

Pranayama is a method of refining the makeup of one's pranic body, one's physical body and also one's mind. In this way it is possible for a practitioner to become aware of new dimensions of existence. By making the mind calm and still, consciousness is allowed to shine through without distortion.

Pranayama has the greatest influence on the mind, for it acts through the pranic body which is more intimately linked to the mind than is the physical body.

One of the main purposes of pranayama is control of one's breath, which leads to control of prana. In turn, control of prana implies control of one's mind. By regulating the flow of prana in the body one can tranquilize the mind and free it, at least for some time, of the incessant conflicts and thoughts that make higher awareness difficult.[28]

In our terminology, becoming "aware of new dimensions of existence" means contact with the Agency—two-way contact. There are three stages of this practice. The first two are preparatory, to get you accustomed to this kind of breathing. They are very easy and are completely safe. The third stage is the real deal and is much harder at first.

If you're up for it.

Preliminary: How to breathe

First, if your nose is blocked it is essential to do *jala neti* (nasal cleansing) prior to practicing pranayama. Even if your nose is reasonably clear it is still beneficial to do *jala neti* prior to your yoga practices. Here's how.

Jala neti is a process of cleaning your nasal passages with salt water, and is essential in allowing free breathing for these practices. It also helps to ensure your good health. Go to a whole foods grocery store or health food store and buy a neti pot—or get one online. This is a

Get a neti pot

small ceramic pot with a long spout. Follow the enclosed directions. Briefly, you fill the pot with lukewarm water, add a pinch of salt, and while tilting your head to one side, you pour the water into one nostril and allow it to run out the other one. This is much easier and much more pleasant to do than your overtime imagination is probably churning right now if you're new to this. My advice is to be brave, get a pot and just do it. Consider this one of those little tests the Agency gives to see if you're serious.

Now comes the breathing. To inhale, expand your diaphragm first, then your upper chest. To exhale, contract your diaphragm first, then your upper chest, like squeezing a toothpaste tube from the bottom up. Never strain at either end of the breath. Breathe slowly and evenly—your breath should always be relaxed. Take your time with these exercises, and keep your awareness on your breath, even later on in Stage 3 when you're counting. So, you are going to breeze right through Stage 1 and Stage 2, described next. After that comes the big one.

Note that being under the influence of drugs or alcohol completely nullifies the benefits of this practice.

Nadi Shodhana – Stage 1

This first exercise is called *Nadi Shodhana* in Sanskrit. *Nadi* means "psychic passage," and *shodhana* means "purification." So this is a practice to purify and decongest the pranic (subtle energy) passages in your body. (It works even if you don't think you have such things.) Sit in a comfortable position, either in a straight-backed chair or in a seated yoga position that keeps your spine straight. Alternatively you can sit on the floor with legs outstretched and back against a wall. Place the first two fingers of your right hand (or left hand, whichever you prefer) to your forehead with you thumb and ring finger alongside either nostril. These are used to alternately press each nostril closed. Your head and back should be upright but without strain.

Close your eyes, relax, and become aware of your breath. Now close your right nostril and slowly inhale and exhale through your left nostril. (This is why your nasal passages must be clear.) Do this for a minute, then open the right nostril and close the left one. Repeat, with awareness of your breath. If your awareness wanders, gently bring it back to your breathing.

Easy.

Stage 2

This is the same as Stage 1, except as follows: First close your right nostril and inhale. Without straining, breathe in deeply using your abdomen and chest to fill your lungs. Now close your left nostril and open your right one. Exhale slowly and empty your lungs as much as possible. Now, still keeping the left nostril closed, inhale back through your right nostril, then switch again and exhale through your left.

We'll go over this again, but this is one round. Inhale through your left nostril and out your right. Then in the right and out the left. Use your index finger and thumb to alternately close each nostril in turn. Don't force or strain your breath in any way. Over time you can slowly increase the duration of your inhalations and exhalations. Nothing extreme, though— no straining. Easy breaths.

Meditation: *Anuloma Viloma* and *Prana Shuddhi*

This meditation is similar to the previous exercises, except the hand position you used on your nose (which is called a *mudra* in yoga) is not used; instead, you sit or lie quietly and mentally imagine that your breath alternately flows through each nostril. It is specifically designed to heighten your awareness and increase your concentration. It is also an important exercise using your imagination, and is a challenge to your ability to remain completely aware of yourself for the entire duration of the exercise. Finally, it is designed to induce a true meditative state if practiced faithfully. This means, Dear Reader, among other things, your mental chatter is gone.

Anuloma viloma means "up and down" or "alternate" in Sanskrit. It is called the coming and going breath. This refers not only to the alternate in and out breathing, but the up and down motion of your awareness from in front of and a little below the nose, up to the center of the forehead and back. *Prana* means breath or subtle breath. The word *shuddhi* means "to purify," so the term means the purifying breath. It's a technique to purify yourself. Not too shabby.

Awareness is your most important asset.

You must insure that you are not interrupted during this practice. This is jarring, and would defeat the entire purpose of doing it. This meditation may be done sitting or lying. I like to lie down as I can more completely relax my entire body. However, it is very easy to fall asleep in this position, so your awareness must remain very sharp throughout. The instructions seem complicated, but it's easy to get the hang of them. I'll get to the really hard part—but the part with the most value—at the end of the description. Here's what you're going to do.

Relax your whole body and close your eyes. Become aware of your breathing. Feel as if nothing else exists but your breath.

First do *anuloma viloma*. Unlike the previous two stages, this is not a physical practice, so don't use your hands to close your nostrils. This is an inner practice, so try to feel that you are breathing in and out of your left nostril. Use your imagination here; imagination leads to execution and reality. Follow the air flow you are aiming for with your attention. At first you *act as if* you are breathing through only one nostril. Eventually, you really will be breathing through only one nostril.

Continue for a minute or two. Then repeat the same thing with your right nostril. Try to feel that the whole flow of your breath moves in and out of your right nostril. Again continue for a minute or two. Remain fully aware of your breathing throughout.

Now use your imagination to control the movement of air through each nostril as you did earlier in Stage 2, but again, don't use your hands. Feel that you are inhaling through your left nostril. Then feel your exhalation through your right nostril. Then back in through your right nostril and out through the left.

This is one round of *anuloma viloma*. Do four rounds.

Now do one round of *prana shuddhi*. This is sometimes called conical breathing, for you imagine the flow of air through both nostrils simultaneously in the form of an inverted "V." In other words, during inhalation the flow of air through both nostrils meets at a point at the center of your eyebrows, and during exhalation the air flow diverges downward from the center of your eyebrows and out your nose. Take a full breath. Both imagination and awareness are required at first.

A single inhalation and exhalation is one round of *prana shuddhi*.

Do four more rounds of *anuloma viloma* and one more round of *prana shuddhi*. Now you've got the hang of the parts of the entire practice, which I'll describe next.

Alternate Breathing with Counting

You're going to mentally count down each round starting from 100 and ending with 0 as follows. 100—one round of *prana shuddhi:* in and out through both nostrils. A very relaxing way to start, so breathe deeply.

99—one round of *anuloma viloma* (breathe in through left, out through right, in through right, out through left nostril). 98—the same thing again. 97, 96, again the same. Then at 95—one round of *prana shuddhi*, breathing in and out through both nostrils, into and out of the eyebrow center. 94, 93, 92, 91—one round each of *anuloma viloma*. 90—one round of *prana shuddhi*. And so on.

To simplify as much a possible, on rounds ending with 0 or 5 you breathe once through both nostrils. For all the other rounds you breathe through alternate nostrils.

It is important not to forget where you are in the counting. Do any mental tricks, visualizations, language reminders or mental activity you can think of to remain aware of the count, your breathing and the movement into and out of your eyebrow center. You'll be busy! You must breathe slowly and steadily, and not try to rush. Also be aware of your body and keep it relaxed. You may pause your breathing for a few moments after any inhalation or exhalation.

Here's the hard part. If your mind wanders and you forget to count or lose your count, then you must start over. You must fight like a warrior to remain alert and not drift off. This is especially apt to happen during a breathing pause. Due to its difficulty, this is truly a combat mission! However, the benefits that may be realized are well worth the effort.

Here is one trick I use to remain alert. Repeating the round number to yourself is important. So I will say to myself, "99 up" during the inhalation through my left nostril. Then, "99 out" during the exhalation out my right nostril. "99 back" during inhalation through my right nostril. Finally, "99 home" as I finish the round by breathing out my left nostril. Don't forget what number you're on! Mentally, make a big deal of counting. Because if you get to 37, say, and your mind wanders away and you can't remember where you were, you have to start over. You have completed the practice when you breathe in and out at the count of zero. At this point, wait silently for a while and see what comes to you on the inner level.

This entire exercise will take about half an hour to forty-five minutes if you start from 100. If pressed for time, or if you just want to ease into it, you may start from 50 or even 25 instead of 100. The benefits won't be as great, though, so shoot for 100 rounds eventually. The mental speaking and counting will help you remain alert. After you have lost count and fallen asleep once or twice and have to start all over, you will learn how to stay alert! The primary purpose of this meditation isn't the healing and other benefits of pranayama (which are wonderful in themselves), but instead is gaining control of your awareness. The side effect is that you will know when the Agency comes calling, because this practice will still your mind. The battleground is between your will and your mind and body. The goal is control of your attention, so your will must prevent your mind from wandering and your body from falling asleep.

With just a little practice these breathing techniques will become second nature; they are easier to do than to describe in words. You will have time to observe yourself and what is happening in your mental sphere. The more strongly you can visualize the movement of your breath as something substantial, the more easily you can remain alert. Don't worry, though, if you lose count. Simply start over. The more you practice the better able you will be able to keep your awareness.

It is all right to pause the breath and counting at either end of the breath; you should try both. But beware! When you still your body's breathing movement, you are most likely to lose your awareness and drift off for a few moments or even fall asleep. But the whole point and power of this exercise is exactly in this moment of extreme stillness, so it is vital that you not lose awareness. The requirement to start over if you lose count or consciousness is the punishment you give yourself every time you lose the battle with yourself.

The Real Game

Things are not okay in the world. Everyone knows this.

Many things could be a lot better. Even though natural disasters seem to be increasing in number and intensity, they are still dwarfed by the disasters of fear, greed, and selfishness we perpetrate on each other. Genocide, ethnic cleansing, war. These are the big things. Petty quarrels, pain, bullying, vindictiveness, loneliness. These are the little things, and we know far too many of both kinds. They are all caused because we are estranged from a greater reality that we can no longer sense—a unity of sufficiency, belonging, proper purpose, love and caring for one another. It's as if we are stranded in personal isolation booths, unable to open the doors and be a part of what's going on outside.

What happened?

A war of control for our lives is also going on, a mostly economic war, because nowadays the old weaponry such as swords, rifles, tanks and warplanes has been largely replaced by financial instruments wielded by psychopathic banks and mega-corporations that fire bullets of debt, poverty, competition, greed, marketing come-on, disenfranchisement and loss that we must continually navigate. Most of us don't even know this is a war, but we as ordinary individuals are the victims of it. Where is liberty, beyond the economic yoke that demands a lifetime of work? When can we stop pursuing happiness and just enjoy it? What, indeed, has become of our lives? (To not know that these questions have very creative, positive answers on both individual and community levels is to have already lost this war.)

There is strong evidence now that a global cataclysm destroyed a Golden Age long ago, or if you prefer, has made the chances for a new one in the here-and-now seemingly impossible. ("A Golden Age?" we ask. "Are you kidding?") But as bad as the physical destruction was, it was nothing compared to the crippling damage it did to our conscious minds. Because of it, we became estranged from a level of reality that a great many people are completely unaware of. Yet it is not some far-off fantasy realm of wishful make-believe. It is an ontological level of existence just over our shoulders—right here—that our consciousness can't quite grasp most of the time. But other times—quiet times—we know that something else might exist …

We now know that an Agency of some kind has sent us a message that there is more to reality than our limited senses tell us. That we might have responsibilities to something beyond ourselves, which are the reasons we're here in this level of reality in the first place. Some contribution we're expected to make. Some evolutionary advance in the universe. Some things only we ourselves can do, were we whole again. This is the message of all the 366, .2732 and 18.6 patterns. Some things we can help the Agency do.

So contacting this Agency is Job One. The only way we are each going to understand what we're here *for* is to reunite with that part of ourselves

Job One from Agencyland

that has become lost across the ontological divide—for the only way we will actually be able to do these further jobs, or even understand what they are, is to reunite with those estranged parts of ourselves that have become lost to our ordinary senses. These two halves of ourselves were symbolized in our earlier argument by the fine structure constant, 137, only being half of our principal pattern number, 273, remembering that half of 273 is 137 (rounded up to a whole number). The half of the Cosmos we see and measure has a counterpart we don't see—symbolized by the missing 137. Agencyland.

If we're in an involuntary game of hide-and-seek here on the Earth of our senses, the fact of which we discovered earlier, we must fully raise our blindfolds and go find that which has been hidden from us. Having now seen the clues left for us—and recognized that in fact they *are* clues—we must play this new game full a-wares. To pretend there is nothing hidden from us—to pretend the patterns we've discovered aren't real, or to pretend there isn't a game afoot—is to stick our heads in the sand, ostrich-like.

In this game of hide-and-seek, the hiding has already been done. Now is the time for seeking. You now have the clues for how to go about this, and they're as clear as if someone had left a bottle labeled "Drink me" on the table. Quiet the mind. Find the place of stillness within. And listen. That's the state of being that is required to discover the next clues in the game. You will discover after not many steps that what is hidden will be found. Then another game can begin, and this *next* game is terrific, because it involves terraforming reality. It is played by rejoining and reuniting with the faeries, divine spirits, gods, goddesses, humans and others who comprise the Agency in a dance that transforms everything.

All you have to do to start playing this game is to show up with your attention, your breath and your awareness. The game can't go on without you—the reunified you. They are waiting for you; they are waiting for us all to get the message and make the effort to find them. If we don't show up and learn to play these new games, the games will move forever beyond our ken and be lost to us. But what is far worse, we will remain estranged and alone, and will never become whole and fulfilled, and a greater sadness than this cannot be imagined.

Figure 19

Appendix – Summary of the Evidence

Here is what we discovered. Within the accuracy of our measurements (three or four significant digits), we have made the following observations:

Number	Occurrence
0.2372	A new constant of the natural world, derived only from a square and an inscribed circle, calculated from the expression $(4 - \pi) / \pi$, using either their areas or perimeters.
3.66	The reciprocal of this number.
0.273	Ratio of Moon to Earth diameters.
3.66	Ratio of Earth to Moon diameters.
400	Ratio of the Sun's diameter to the Moon's diameter. Also the Sun is 400 times farther from Earth than the Moon is.
366	Number of full rotations of the Earth in one year.
27.32	The sidereal period (and length of day) of the Moon, expressed in Earth days.
10,000	The number of Earth days in 366 lunar days.
273.2°K	The freezing point of water on the Kelvin scale. (equals 0° Centigrade)
273	Average human gestation period in days.
27+	Average feminine menstrual cycle in days.
1/273.2	From the ideal gas law: the fraction of their volume gasses expand or contract per degree Centigrade at a constant pressure.
2.73°K	The temperature of the cosmic microwave background radiation.
.273	The square root of the ratio of the sidereal periods of the Moon and the Earth.
109.3	The number of Earths that fit side-by-side in the Sun.
109.3	The number of Suns that fit in the Earth's orbital radius. 4 x 27.32 = 109.28—sensibly the same number.

Number	Occurrence
109.91	The reciprocal of 0.9099, which is 1.0991, multiplied by 100. 0.9099 is derived from the surface areas (or volumes) of a cube and an inscribed sphere, using the expression $(6 - \pi) / \pi$.
7920	The diameter of Earth in miles. Also 8 x 9 x 10 x 11.
2160	The diameter of the Moon in miles. Also 8 x 9 x 10 x 3.
5040	The sum of the radius of the Earth (3960) and Moon (1080) in miles. Also 7 x 8 x 9 x 10 and 7!, which is shorthand for 1 x 2 x 3 x 4 x 5 x 6 x 7.
8640	1/100 the diameter of the Sun in miles. Also 8 x 9 x 10 x 12. it is an approximate number, as the Sun doesn't have a well-defined diameter.
$12^5/10$	The mean circumference of the Earth in miles. It equals 24,883.2 miles, which is 99.99% of the currently accepted value.
86,400	The number of seconds in one mean solar day (exactly 24 hours). Also one tenth the diameter of the Sun in miles.
86,164	The number of seconds in one sidereal day. This is 236 seconds shorter than a mean solar day.
.273	The percent difference between a sidereal day and a mean solar day (236/86,400 = .273%)
186,300	c, the number of miles light travels per second in a vacuum.
186,300,000	The diameter of Earth's orbit, in miles (canonical value from the range 182.8 to 189 million miles).
1,000	Number of seconds light takes to cross this distance.
18.6	The Earth's velocity around the Sun, in miles per second (canonical value from the range 18.2 to 18.8). Also 1/10,000 the speed of light in miles per second.
2,730,000	The circumference of the Sun in miles, using 870,000 miles as its diameter.
273	The speed in miles per second of a hypothetical planet orbiting the Sun at its surface, according to Kepler's third law.

Number	Occurrence
18.6	The period in Earth years for the Moon's nodes to turn through 360°.
26,000±	The estimated distance in light years to the center of the Milky Way. Canonical value would be 27,320, which is within the statistical range.
26,000±	The number of years Earth's axis precesses through 360°. Canonical value would again be 27,320, as the number cannot be measured accurately in any substantially shorter time frame.
1/137	Known in physics as the fine structure constant, it is a dimensionless number called alpha, which is equal to $e^2 / \hbar c$. Two times 137 is 274, which is just .366% over our number 273.
27.3	The Carrington rotational period of sunspots in Earth days.
27.3	In Hertz, one of the atmospheric Schumann resonant frequencies, the strongest of which is 7.83 Hz. Two octaves above 27.3 hz is 109 Hz.

NOTES

1. Plichta, Peter. *God's Secret Formula*. Shaftsbury, Dorset, England: Element Books, 1997, p. 138.

2. There is much more to be found along these lines in *The Privileged Planet* by Guillermo Gonzalez and Jay Richards. Washington DC: Regnery Publishing, 2004.

3. Our orientation to the galactic center in Sagittarius does play a definite role in my Fool's Journey material. See TheFoolsJourney.net for more details.

4. Lederman, Leon. *The God Particle: If the universe is the answer, what is the question?*. New York: Delta/Dell, 1993, p. 28. For more fascinating information on 137 see *137: Jung, Pauli, and the Pursuit of a Scientific Obsession* by Arthur I. Miller, New York: Norton, 2009.

5. Knight, Christopher and Alan Butler. *Civilization One*. London: Watkins Publishing, 2004.

6. Michel, John. *The Dimensions of Paradise*. Kempton, IL: Adventures Unlimited Press, 2001, p. 24.

7. Cited in Michell, John, *The Dimensions of Paradise*, p. 48.

8. Barrow, John and Frank Tipler. *The Anthropic Cosmological Principle*. New York: Oxford University Press, 1986, p. 2.

9. Gonzalez, Guillermo and Jay Richards, p. 137.

10. Op. cit. p. 263.

11. Like, say, in the Big Bang theory.

12. For more information on these topics, search online for "EPR experiment" or "quantum entanglement." A very readable source is *The Holographic Universe* by Michael Talbot. New York: HarperPerennial, 1992. Another is *Biocentrism* by Robert Lanza. Dallas: Benbella, 2009.

13. Buckminster Fuller. *Synergetics*. New York: MacMillan, 1975, p. xxxi.

14. Lynne McTaggart. *The Intention Experiment*. New York: Free Press, 2007, Chapter 11, "Praying for Yesterday."

15. Op. cit. p. 165.

16. One resource to get a feel for this idea is *The Goldilocks Enigma* by Paul Davies. New York: Houghten Mifflin, 2006. It is difficult, though, to tell exactly what theories Davies believes himself. On the one hand he acknowledges several alternative theories, even backward causation (p. 243). On the other hand he can say that there is no life force and "Living organisms are machines." (p. 224) He seems deeply conflicted, as many physicists must be right now.

17. Allan, D. S. and J. B. Delair. *Cataclysm! Compelling Evidence of a Cosmic Catastrophe in 9500 BC.* Rochester, VT: Bear & Co., 1997.

18. Evans-Wentz, W. Y.. *The Fairy Faith in Celtic Countries.* New York: University Books, 1994, p. 61.

19. The CD is called *Memories of Home*, and is available from iTunes, CD Baby or LightBridgeMusic.com, my website, where much more information on ancient music is available.

20. See MaltaTemples.com – Sound Phenomenon, a site of the Old Temples Study Foundation.

21. Ibid. See also http://popular-archaeology.com/issue/march-2012/article/the-ancient-architects-of-sound for more details.

22. See the companion site to this book, InvisibleAgentsOfCreation,com, for some sounds you can experience for yourself, plus much more on creating altered states naturally without drugs.

23. More information is available on Wikipedia on these pages: Ionosphere, Schumann Resonance, and Frequency Following Response. A broader discussion is available in *The Resonance Key* by Marie D. Jones and Larry Flaxman. Franklin Lakes, NJ, New Page Books, 2009.

24. For example, see Valerie Hunt's excellent book *Infinite Mind: The Science of Human Vibrations.* Malibu, CA: Malibu Publishing, 1995.

25. http://en.wikipedia.org/wiki/The_Hum. I kid you not.

26. More information is available at the Taos Hum Homepage, http://amasci.com/hum/hum1.html.

27. Check this book's companion website InvisibleAgentsOfCreation,com to see how this research is going.

28. Saraswati, Swami Satyananda. *Yoga & Kriya.* Bihar, India: Yoga Publications Trust, 1981, p. 110-114.

About the author

Fred Cameron is a researcher and lecturer. After earning a joint degree in astronomy and physics, he was hired as a programmer at IBM, and later ran a small software company for many years. Struck by a lack of meaning, he experienced a mid-life crisis and in 1989 had a spiritual awakening which led him to explore different realities beyond the one science describes. He became part of the New Age movement, but found it also lacked essential meaning. So he set out to discover what genuine spiritual truths might still exist in this modern day—a task that lasted twelve years and spanned the Western Hermetic tradition, Sufism, and several Eastern traditions. From this work he developed the Fool's Journey, a synthesis of perennial spiritual teachings, which will appear in a forthcoming book, *The Fool's Secret Journey*. *Invisible Agents of Creation* is one approach to this material for those not especially religious or even spiritual. He gives workshops and teaches classes on these and related subjects.

Mr. Cameron recorded a CD of original music, *Memories of Home*, using ancient tunings from Sumer that date back five thousand years. *Invisible Agents of Creation* is his second book. He lives near Seattle, Washington, and does not like talking about himself in the third person.

Discover the latest research,
order more copies of this book or the ebook,
and take part in the discussion.

Visit this book's companion website
InvisibleAgentsOfCreation.com

or the author's website

FredCameron.com

Made in the USA
Charleston, SC
09 October 2014